To Jo
Best
Steve
2008

CW01431313

Letting Go

Taking Control by Letting Go

Steve Unwin

A 'Change-ability' title

Photon Books
www.photonbooks.com

Published by Photon Books 2008
First published in Great Britain in 2007
www.photonbooks.com

Printed and bound in Great Britain.

ISBN 978-1-906420-00-0

Printed by Biddles, Kings Lynn
www.biddles.co.uk

ATEBIDPC3.0

To Us All

When you have an idea – who does it belong to?

We are each the product of our connections to everyone we have known. In turn those we have known are the product of their own connections. As fibres of the same web we are all a product of us all.

In each of us, we see all of us.

Contents

Acknowledgements

'All things are bound together.
All things connect.
What happens to the Earth, happens to the children of the Earth.
People have not woven the Web of life.
Each is but one thread.
Whatever we do to the Web,
we do to ourselves.'
Chief Seattle.

To produce anything draws on the countless connections which form our understanding of the world and what we are within it.

The process of writing a book underlines just how important these connections, whether long term or fleeting, really are.

Many of those who have helped in the creation of this book, did so indirectly and often unwittingly. I would like to thank them all. They have each shaped a thought, coloured a feeling, given texture to an idea and created the palette from which I have drawn.

I harbour the hope that I have, even if unwittingly, given back a small part of what they gave me.

All have helped make this book possible.

Thank you.

Special thanks to Dave Yarrow and Eileen Murray who each inspired me to continue, when it seemed easier not to, and to Lorna Davidson without whom the journey would not have begun.

Extra special thanks to my family for their understanding, patience, support and love, and without whom the journey would have been a lonely one.

Also with very grateful thanks to fellow travellers whose words I have quoted throughout the book.

Change-ability

In a world of incessant change there are no answers, only questions; nothing we must do, only things we must be. Change therefore is not an activity, but an ability.

'Before you can break out of prison, you must first realize you're locked up.'
Anon

There is no doubt that we find change uncomfortable, so much so that we expend great effort avoiding its demands and denying its imperative. Even acceptance of change is tendered with ill grace. Resentfully when pushed we shift our feet but only with a view to secure another stable position. We have been moved, but are not movement, we change where we are, but not what we are, we change what we do, but not what we are being. In short we seek to change without being changed.

But our world provides no stable positions. We live our lives on shifting sheets of ice where there is no standing still. What we do is fixed at a point in time, but our world is not. What works now in this moment, may not in the next. Answers, however well they serve the present, are trapped in time and die and decay like the fashion they are. We need questions with which to transcend the passing moment we call 'now', and be in the travelling current moment that is 'now'.

A world of questions denies our feet the apparent security and comfort of firm ground.

'Life is either a daring adventure, or nothing. Security does not exist in nature, nor do the children of men as a whole experience it. Avoiding danger is no safer in the long run than exposure.'
Helen Keller

It is easy for the anxious energy this creates to live as fear, and drive us to seek security even where we know it cannot exist. However if we understand the liberation we have been given, this very same energy can fuel our flight. We are no longer trapped in the past, but free to explore the infinite opportunities of our every next step.

There are no answers, however much we crave them, and so this book offers none.

I hope however that it may help you create your own living questions to guide your path across your shifting ice.

This book is the first in a series, each helping illuminate the challenge of change-ability, like fragments of mosaic from which you can create your own pictures.

I hope you enjoy your journey through the book. If you would like to share your comments and thoughts I would love to hear from you. Please email lettinggo@photonbooks.com.

Steve Unwin,
July 2008.

Introduction

When I was young I had it drummed into me that books were to be cherished, cared for and treated with respect. I learned never to open the pages too forcefully, never to fold over the corner of the page, and never, ever to write in a book. If you were taught like I was, then for this book I ask you to make an exception. Have a pen with which to mark the book, scribble, annotate, underline, strike through, re-write and do whatever to turn this from my book, into your book; a book with your thoughts and ideas.

Thinking

Let me take a moment to explain why this is so important.

If you've ever seen a picture of a human brain you may have noted that our brains are divided into two quite separate halves. This separation is not simply a cosmetic physical division, rather we might more appropriately think of having two connected but quite distinct brains. Each works in such a profoundly different way, that there is little exaggeration in saying that we have two quite different people living in our heads.

Perhaps mischievously, our brains are cross wired to our body; the left brain taking the lead in controlling the right side, whilst the right brain leads control of the left side. The prevalence of right handed people in part reflects the dominance of the left brain.

Logic

Our left brain's functioning is the most familiar to most of us. It is based on logic and sequences, processing information in a serial manner, starting at the beginning, working through the middle and on to the end. Our left brain sees the world and everything in it through this structured framework. As a consequence it is particularly good at tasks that require this sequential processing, such as language tasks like reading this book, and mathematics, for example performing the calculation, '2 + 5 ='.

When we see the character '2' our left brain recognises and understands two, and sees it as the start of a calculation.

It sees the character '+' and now knows what sort of a calculation to perform. It understands

'5' and is ready for work, and the symbol '=' is the signal to start the work through which our left brain will in most cases successfully deliver the answer 7.

This is a trivial example of an incredibly powerful and valuable capability which we make use of all the time, and without which we couldn't have created the world we now live in. But this isn't the only way for a brain to work, and we know this for certain, because it's not the way our right brain works.

In fact our right brain is profoundly different. Where the left brain works serially, we might think of the right brain working in a parallel fashion, dealing with lots of pieces of information at the same time rather than sequentially. When it sees '2 + 5 =', it doesn't see this as a sequence at all. Instead it sees the elements all together as a kind of pattern of shapes and sets off to discover some meaning from them. To our left brain this of course seems pretty dumb. It's obvious to it that the sequence is significant and reads left to right. We've seen this type of sequence many times, and without the sequence it makes no sense, it's just a set of shapes.

Our left brain's singular ability to serially process is very valuable when this is what's required, but it is blind to other processing possibilities. Our left brain is therefore often quick to dismiss the right brain as ineffective, or just fails to understand it at all. Our left brain knows the correct way to process information and is blind to its blindness of other ways.

You (in the guise of your dominant left brain) might already find yourself arguing that our left brain is correct, and that failing to see this as a task of addition *is* just dumb. However let me illustrate the value of this parallel processing.

Imagine a large set of 1024 different numbers. In fact let's imagine not just one but 768 such sets, i.e. 786,432 different numbers, (1024 x 768).

Let's now consider the possible values of each of those numbers. Our left brain might be hoping that we keep the values small to simplify the maths, but no such luck. Let's say the numbers can be in the range 0 to 4,294,967,296.

Our left brain is in meltdown. It imagines that if we simply add the numbers together, and each addition takes only five seconds, this processing will take over 45 days, of continuous effort. This is a massive task for our left brain! Yet we might be surprised to know that our right brain, with its parallel approach of seeing them all together, processes the equivalent information not in 45 days or even 45 seconds, but in an instant, indeed it is doing it all of the time, and of course your brain is doing it now.

How?

Imagine your computer screen, or a photograph taken with a digital camera. The picture you see is typically 1024 pixels wide and 768 pixels high, (786,432 pieces of information) and each pixel can have four thousand million different values (32 binary bits), yet you instantly recognise a picture of your child, the Eiffel Tower or the Mona Lisa for example. What's more, you don't simply recognise your child, but you probably recall the day the picture was taken, what was happening, how you felt. The trip to Paris; what you saw; where you ate. In a fraction of a second you have processed this immense amount of data, created understanding, and built new information to add to it.

Remarkably the right brain, which fails even to recognise the task of our simple addition, let alone calculate the answer, excels at this 'parallel' processing task.

Computers

The laptop on which I'm writing this text, works much like our left brain, largely processing information serially. Computers are incredibly fast performing millions of operations each second, vastly superior to our human brain's few hundred operations per second. However even the most powerful computers struggle to match the ability of our right brain to perform the immense amount of analysis required to recognise someone's face viewed from any angle. This recognition problem is not a problem of processing speed, but of processing approach, or what we as humans might call thinking style. Our right brain's parallel processing approach is what is required.

Dominance

Both brains are of course extremely valuable and provide powerful tools, but perhaps because our left brain deals with mathematics, and more importantly language, processing the words you are reading now in much the same serial way as the simple calculation above, our left brain thinking is dominant. It's the way most of us recognise the communication of ideas. As a consequence, it is the way in which we think of thinking and of problem solving. Indeed we might argue that computers have been built in our image of what we think thinking comprises. As a consequence, for most of us our logical left brain dominates our thinking and understanding as individuals, and also dominates the style of thinking we have as a society, at least in western cultures.

We associate our left brain with the task of thinking. We recognise the effort expended on tasks such as mathematics, and place a value on this and what it achieves. Paradoxically rather than reflecting our ability, this sense of value more often reflects the difficulty we experience with these logical tasks.

There are only 10 different kinds of people in the world: those who know binary and those who don't.
Anon.

Our right brain in contrast, performs so effortlessly that we scarcely notice it doing anything at all. From the moment we wake up, it is processing vast amounts of data to understand its surroundings, recognise objects, calculate their position and relationships, understand images. All this in order to see the time on the alarm clock that disturbed your sleep! There's nothing in this activity that we could call work, certainly nothing that can be recognised as such by our left brain and thus nothing to which we can attach credit. We barely recognise this alternate form of thinking taking place and far less appreciate what it comprises or how it works.

Intuition

For many, perhaps the perfect insult is for our logical left brain to call our right brain artistic, intuitive or creative, describing an illogical, random process reliant on good fortune. To our right brain 'intuition' takes on a completely different meaning that is difficult to describe in words, as those words will be written and read by our serial processing left brain.

We need to think of a single photographic image to grasp the incomprehension of our left brain. Faced with the prospect of over 45 days of processing, an immediate response can only be seen as magic, an illusion, or an act of purest chance. Interpreting 786,432 pieces of data as Niagara Falls, Nelson Mandela, the surface of the Moon, a Model T Ford or the face of our child, can scarcely be explained in any other way. Our left brain knows that the answer can't have been arrived at by what it understands to be a valid logical process.

However described, the feat has the air of the charlatan, and is dismissed as invalid. Yet we know it is not luck or chance. We know with absolute certainty what the picture describes. We know we are correct. Even though we don't know how we do it, we know that we do it.

This parallel processing is so commonplace that we don't attach the word 'intuition' to our understanding of pictures. However we do reserve the word for the many other forms of understanding which does not follow the serial approach of our left brain. Each is viewed at the very least with deep suspicion when evaluated using the framework of logic.

Although something of a mystery to our dominant left brain, we make a grave mistake if we dismiss or fail to recognise the remarkable power of our intuition.

'The artist is a receptacle for emotions that come from all over the place: from the sky, from the earth, from a scrap of paper, from a passing shape...'
Pablo Picasso

We need to value both types of thinking if we are to succeed. The logic of our left brain is a powerful tool to dissect and analyse. It lets us look in great detail at sections of our world, to understand its composition and ingredients. Without it you could not be working your way through this text to read this book, processing word by word and page by page recognising the patterns of words you've seen many times before. However it is our right brain that sees new big pictures, connects these pieces together, along with pieces from elsewhere, to create a coherent whole. Crucially it is our right brain that cries 'ah-ha' when things suddenly make sense, and where the excitement of revelation and the magic of understanding takes place.

Books

Returning now to the nature of this book, a book about creating change, creating the future. When anticipating such a book, our left brain naturally seeks to see and understand through a logical structure. It wants to be told. It wants a book that starts at the beginning, runs through the middle, and ties everything up neatly before reaching the conclusion. Our left brain wants to see the book as complete, as finished, as something to be read, as something to be preserved in its completed and clean state. More than this, it wants a book of answers, instructions to follow, themselves with a start, a middle and an end. Yet this need cannot be

'It's a damn poor mind that can think of only one way to spell a word.'
Andrew Jackson

satisfied. The future can't be known, it's not a place of answers, instead a place of questions with which to illuminate what will become. So our left brain's search must switch from a book of answers to a book of questions.

But in the hands of answer seekers, even a book of questions soon becomes a checklist to follow and itself a form of answers. To enable our right brain to create understanding we need to generate our own pictures, not simply view those drawn by others. Our right brain needs to make connections, to process information in parallel, perhaps otherwise disjointed and dissimilar pieces of information. Snippets taken from experience, picked up from conversations, half remembered discussions, ideas developed in quite different contexts. It needs to amalgamate these things that may have no logical serial connections at all, no matter how rapidly or feverishly processed by our left brain, or left brain styled computers. Our right brain takes these fragments, shards of glass, and by a process we might reasonably call magic, luck or intuition, creates rich pictures of vivid new understanding.

'When you make the finding yourself - even if you're the last person on Earth to see the light - you'll never forget it.'
Carl Sagan

This is not the left brain process of slotting together the pieces in sequence to calculate a result, but the creation of a new way of seeing and connecting. It doesn't simply enable us to produce a new result, it creates change within us; we are changed by the new understanding.

Under-standing

We need not a detailed description of the match, nor a treatise on how it functions. Rather we need to become the heat of its flame. We need to become questions.

'Discovery consists of looking at the same thing as everyone else does and thinking something different.'
Albert Szent-Gyorgyi,

Thus your thoughts and understanding are the sole purpose of this book. How you are changed by having read, not what you have read, is its purpose.

Your thoughts need cultivation and this means creating the right mood in which to create them, and then capturing them before they are lost. You need to allow yourself to be receptive, allow your mind to wander, and be prepared to listen to what it finds.

Whilst our left brain looks to fit things into what it knows, it is our right brain that looks at things askance, makes sometimes bizarre and insightful connections to see in new ways. We need to quieten our dominant left brain, so that we can hear what our right brain may be whispering.

'Sometimes we are afraid to question because we confuse it with doubt, at times when doubt cannot be indulged. Continued…

I'm sure you will have your own thoughts for creating the relaxed mood for this thinking. One of the hardest pressures to deal with is that voice

... continued. Questioning is not the same thing. Living the questions requires a willingness to live with paradox, to endure confusion in our rational minds that only the intuitive mind can entertain: intuition accepts the paradox instead of changing it.' Christina Baldwin

that says you should be doing something else. To help with this, I've made the book short. Not so you can fit it into a heavy schedule, for awareness of the schedule will lurk in the background and disable your freedom. Rather it is short to help you dispel any thought of schedule. Of course I hope that if it stimulates your thinking, the real benefit will be found outside the book and the quotations are designed to invite these excursions of thought.

I've left plenty of space on the pages for you to capture your thoughts. These may appear in an instant and can disappear just as quickly, like the dream that rapidly fades even as we try to frame it in the first moments of waking day. When we try to capture our thoughts in words, we need our linguistic left brain to help, yet the act of transferring our thinking from right to left can destroy the very pictures we seek to preserve. So don't be afraid to scribble or sketch.

This Book

This book is an example of the work of the intuitive right brain.

In my early writing attempts, though I failed to realise it, my left brain was at the computer keyboard, attempting to describe ideas in a neat sequential manner with a start a middle and an end. Yet each writing brought new learning and the neat pattern was repeatedly destroyed. A book was written, rewritten and rewritten again in search of an elusive completion, yet the process of each rewrite sowed the seeds for the next.

Several years into the project and with mountains of writing, but nothing I could call a book, I found myself listening to my intuition. Maybe I was tired, maybe desperate, maybe I'd run out of other options, but I listened and found myself taking a five week break in Portugal where I would finally complete the project.

I set off to spend the time alone in a hotel on the Portuguese Algarve travelling with what I affectionately called the Zimmer Frame Set on a special discount winter deal, and became the rather strange chap they saw at mealtimes and who then disappeared to write.

During the first week I tried but achieved nothing. I didn't feel too bad. I needed time to settle in, find my feet and clear my mind. The second week I would begin in earnest and sat each day trying to format the mass of material I'd produced previously and taken with me. However I found that the more I tried, the less it would yield to being shaped and completed.

Two weeks were used up now, 40% gone, the half way point approaching. I could feel the panic welling up within me, a growing numbing debilitating pressure.

The third week; still nothing constructive, lots of scribbles and deletions, a looming sense of impending failure, and desperate long walks on the beach questioning why I was there, and why I was failing. Then towards the end of the third week I found that I had put to one side the reams of prepared material, and had begun to write a story. Over the next five days I wrote the outline for this and a second book.

I write entirely to find out what I'm thinking, what I'm looking at, what I see and what it means.
Joan Didion

I'm not sure where the stories came from. They certainly reflect some of the ideas my left brain had been struggling unsuccessfully to describe, but I had no idea that I was going to write them until I began, and no idea what I would write until it had been written. It seemed that the stories were written by my right brain, and the best way I could help was to keep my left brain from making too many interruptions. My right brain isn't able to explain how they were written, and my left brain of course has no option but to see them as a product of chance, magic or intuition. The result is a quite different approach to that of my left brain. Rather than describe my ideas of change I hope it invites you to create your own ideas and your own understanding.

Sharing

Although we speak to each other through these sequential words, left brain to left brain, I hope each will act as a messenger to link our right brains together to share and create new pictures and new understanding.

The changing world we live in is a connected place full of interactions and parallel activities. It is a place often little understood by our left brain which is continuously bemused as its calculations of the future prove woefully incorrect, and its neat serial understanding is repeatedly swept aside by the apparent unfathomable complexities of real world interactions.

The world is a place to be understood by the right brain, and change is a right brain activity.

We all indulge in the strange, pleasant process called thinking, but when it comes to saying, even to someone opposite, what we think, then how little we are able to convey! The phantom is through the mind and out of the window before we can lay salt on its tail, or slowly sinking and returning to the profound darkness which it has lit up momentarily with a wandering light.

Virginia Woolf, Thought and Thinking

Quotations

Throughout the book you'll see that I've included quotations that I've found resonate with my own feelings and for me elegantly reflect the ideas I hope to share.

The quotations have been selected solely for their resonance; for what was said, rather than who said it. I am heartened to observe that the quotations come from such a diverse population.

'We all write poems; it is simply that the poets are the ones who write in words.'
John Fowles

You may wish to read the story first ignoring the quotations, so as not to interrupt the flow, or perhaps just read the quotations to create your own story, or maybe approach the book some other way. In any event the choice is yours. It's your story now, so take it where you will and follow where it leads.

Steve Unwin

Letting Go

'I find it fascinating that most people plan their vacations with better care than they plan their lives. Perhaps that is because escape is easier than change.'
Jim Rohn

We all face the inescapable challenge of change. Though we may desperately try to ignore the fact, from the moment we are born the world around us, even the body we live within, is constantly undergoing change. It is the one constant in our lives.

Our story concerns three animals; donkey, beetle and cat. Of themselves they were quite unremarkable, just typical folk living the kind of regular lives you might expect of such animals.

The three had become perhaps unlikely friends as they shared their lives on the steeply sloping sides of a small mountain.

One thing before we begin their story; it may help to know that when animals say 'folk' they mean animals with any number of legs, or even those with no legs at all, such as fish or worms. When they say 'people' they mean just the two legged animals like you or I.

Whispered

Donkey worked for a mining company which exploited a minor seam of precious metal that many years previously had been discovered on the surface, and since then had been pursued as it burrowed deep within the mountain's heart. Like many, donkey's contribution perhaps seemed small in the greater scheme of things, helping to carry supplies to the miners across terrain that proved too difficult for the company's vehicles. The land around the mine was scarred with ravines and pock marked with holes, some natural and many man-made by previous workings to extract the mountain's riches.

Letting Go

Roused each morning from his small paddock near the foot of the mountain, donkey would move supplies from a storage base up to the mine entrance. From there the supplies would be offloaded and taken inside the mine, deep inside the mountain on trucks clanking their way along narrow rail tracks. Back and forth he would carry supplies, weaving his precarious way along barely defined mountain paths. Four, five, sometimes six times each day he'd make the arduous journey, interspersed with breaks, when there was time to eat, drink and even sometimes to think and talk with friends.

The first of these friends, beetle, quite naturally did beetle like things, scurrying here and there and generally busying himself in a beetly sort of way. Always appearing busy, beetle had his own concerns and tasks to complete. Not least of these were maintaining his nest, or 'accommodation' as he liked to call it, and finding food.

The last of our trio was cat. For the moment he had turned his back on the comforts of domesticity and had chosen the freedom of the mountain. He was a friend to the miners when it suited, and free to roam when it didn't. The miners had adopted him as the 'mine cat', a sort of lucky mascot or so it seemed. Cat had some previous experience of this type of human

'For a long time it seemed to me that real life was about to begin, but there was always some obstacle in the way. Something had to be got through first, some unfinished business; time still to be served, a debt to be paid. Then life would begin. At last it dawned on me that these obstacles were my life.'
Bette Howland.

delusion and saw no reason to disabuse the miners of it, for the time being at least. The position of 'mine cat' had its perks, and the duties he felt only the slightest obligation to fulfil, were hardly onerous; some timely purring, affectionate rubbing against the miners' legs from time to time when they emerged from the darkness of the mine, and allowing the miners to stroke the back of his neck whilst being fed titbits. The real work, such as it was, concerned keeping the food supplies free from the attention of any errant mice. However these appeared quite rarely, and the work when it arrived was so pleasurable that cat barely considered it to be work at all. 'This would do currently', cat had thought to himself when he allowed the miners to think he had accepted the role, 'whilst I consider other career options'.

The three lived their lives, normal, unexceptional lives, on the steep sides of the mountain. Days came and passed with little in the way of major drama or incident. Ours is not a story of major cataclysm, a mining disaster, land slide or earthquake. Rather it is the story of the ordinary events of ordinary lives. Indeed that is a key point of our tale. Whilst the nature of stories is often to focus on the dramatic, the rare and sensational, in the main our lives are led in the middle ground of days free from these extremes. If we forget this, we may find our time has been all used up whilst we were waiting for the dramatic and were blind to what was happening around us.

Whilst undeniably change sometimes comes dressed with headlines and drama, in the main it seeps into our lives, not with a bang but with a whisper. But it is none the less powerful for this. It is an incessant and ever advancing whisper that continuously but almost invisibly shifts our situations, undermines our assumptions and rewrites our futures, quietly opening and closing doors with each and every moment that passes.

'Life is made of millions of moments, but we live only one of these moments at a time. As we begin to change this moment, we begin to change our lives.'
Trinidad Hunt

Change disguises its incessant work with the occasional loud crash of a major event, but like the gentle erosion of water against rock, change's most profound work is done not when it draws our attention to it, but at quiet times whilst we are looking but not seeing. The challenge of real change is therefore not played to the sound of these brief bursts of energy, the crashing of the cymbals, but to the long periods of deceptive tranquillity.

'We see things not as they are but as we are.'
Anais Nin

As a consequence it is not the way we deal with extreme events that in the most part determines the direction and quality of our lives, but the way we think and behave on these ordinary days, dealing with the steady current of change; the ordinary days which when combined describe our lives.

Steve Unwin

Day One

Warm Inside

We join the friends on a sunny summer day. It's the kind of day that warms you, not just on the outside but on the inside too. The kind of day that seems to say, 'this is what life is for'.

The air is warm and the mood relaxing. Above occasional puffy white clouds decorate the blue of the sky, without the thought of obscuring the sun. There's the scent of flowers to awaken your nose, and you're aware of the buzzing of insects playing a quiet soundtrack to the unfolding scene. It is a day that tickles the senses. In every direction, life of all kinds is proclaiming, 'it's good to be alive!'

Donkey has completed four runs carrying supplies and is quietly hoping that he will soon be taken back down the mountain with his day's work done. He and beetle are enjoying the warm glow of the sun in a field alongside the supply base, whilst they relax and converse in an idle and contented way that perfectly suits the mood of the day. Cat has apparently been on mouse patrol, checking the miners' supplies in the nearby storage hut. After a brief input into the conversation, mainly to enquire about the availability of food, he has now curled himself up to doze in the shade cast by a nearby hawthorn bush. Meanwhile donkey and beetle are sharing some general chit chat about the day.

News

Amongst the idle chatter about the weather, the relative quality of the grass in the adjoining fields and things brought to mind by the shapes of the clouds floating above, donkey adds something to change the conversation's direction. He casually mentions a comment overheard from a discussion between two of the miners.

"… yes, something about the seam getting too thin to be worked … not economical until they can break through. That's what they were saying."

The course of the mine workings, winding their way in the trail of the seam of ore, had hit a particularly hard and barren section of rock that was proving difficult to break through. This was not a totally unusual situation, and similar problems had been encountered several times before in the history of the mine. In all likelihood it would slow progress for a few weeks, after which the seam would be re-established and work would return to normal.

To donkey's ear the comment had simply been something he'd record, as it might later be a welcome input to conversations hungry for something new to discuss. He'd noted it with little comprehension of its potential impact, or as it proved, little suspicion of the impact that beetle would attach to it.

Beetle had heard other comments made by the miners during the previous week and had already begun to worry on donkey's behalf about what they may mean to him.

"Not economical, that's serious!" says beetle momentarily breaking off from exploring the contours of a small grey pebble with his antennae. "You know what that means don't you?"

Donkey is taken unawares by beetle's reaction, not having given much thought beyond recalling the original conversation. He is initially unable to bluff his way through an answer,

"Yes of course, it um .... well not really."

"It means the mine could be closing." There was an unsettling tone of finality in beetle's voice.

"You sure?" said donkey not yet grasping the implications, yet attempting to express a level of concern to reflect that clearly shown by beetle.

"Whenever people talk about economical you can bet that something's going to change, and it usually means closing not opening, stopping not starting."

Beetle raised the tone of his voice as he completed his pronouncement, as if to underline that he was speaking from painful experience.

"Oh closing the mine, well it's only a possibility and anyway ...." Donkey's bluffing abilities were beginning to recover from the initial shock.

"You seem to be taking this all in your stride." Beetle didn't quite know whether to be impressed or alarmed at donkey's unexpectedly relaxed state.

"Well it always seems best not to overreact to news like..." donkey had still not identified a reason to be as concerned as beetle clearly was, but thought he'd buy some time by moving his bluffing up a level, to feigning aloof comprehension.

"If the mine closes that'll be the end for you." Beetle sought to drive home his point.

The word 'end' had a pointedness to it that began to prod at donkey's thinking.

"If they close the mine they won't need you will they?" Beetle emphasised the word 'you' with a nod and the raising of his, admittedly tiny, beetly eyebrows.

'End' and 'won't need you' together chimed a growing note of concern. But donkey had always been all right; things had always worked out. He was a good worker, worked well, diligently and hardly complained at the difficulties thrown at him. Well ok, so the complaining part wasn't totally true, but he reasoned that his complaints had always been reasonable and justified, given the nature of his work.

Change

Beetle continued to paint the bleak picture for donkey.

"If the mine closes things are going to change around here for you donkey."

Beetle was still banging on about this news as if it was some sort of revelation. His words rattled around donkey's head for a moment as he struggled to understand quite why he'd attached so much importance to them … and then he had it!

"Change? Change! Is that it, things are going to change? Is that what you're worrying about beetle? Change?"

"Change big time!" With a grave nod of the head beetle confirmed that donkey had understood the core of the message.

'Truth is eternal, knowledge is changeable. It is disastrous to confuse them.' Madeleine L'Engle

Donkey didn't simply feel the anxiety of incomprehension removed, but felt it replaced by the warm comforting glow that he actually understood the situation much better than beetle. His whole body relaxed. Where he had been drowning, his feet now touched the bottom of the pool. He felt safe.

"Don't worry on my account beetle" said donkey, the last traces of uncertainty fading away, replaced by a warm flush of confidence. "Change is second nature to me. I'm always dealing with change. Every day I carry different things, sometimes tools, sometimes food, sometimes tools and food. It's always changing. Sometimes four times a day, others five and even maybe six. It's all the same to me. I can handle whatever they throw at me. Adaptable that's what I am, always ready to change to fit in with what's required..."

Beetle barely succeeded in stifling a bellow of laughter when he saw the earnest way in which donkey continued his self commendation of his change abilities.

"... Whatever happens to that mine they are always going to need miners and miners are always going to need supplies. What they'll need is adaptable folk who can fit in to whatever changed circumstances they have."

Who Me?

Beetle wasn't sure whether he had provoked the popping of a huge previously untapped bubble of self justification that donkey had kept welled up within him, or whether donkey was desperately trying to convince himself that everything would be ok. In any event, whichever was the case, he felt donkey had some learning to do, and perhaps quickly.

His friend however showed no signs of ending his monologue.

"... maybe it's for the good, I can get the stables improved, they're draughty in winter, and this harness could do with replacing." He shook his head convulsively as if to draw attention to the deficiencies of the harness.

"Whoa there, just slow down a minute," beetle was thinking on his feet how to let donkey down slowly. "Tell me donkey, what is it that you see as your best quality at dealing with change."

Donkey's reply carried more than a hint of frustration as he flicked at some lose earth with a hoof,

"Well I've just been saying. I'm adaptable, proven record of doing things differently, tools, food, you name it."

'The harder you fight to hold on to specific assumptions, the more likely there's gold in letting go of them.'
John Seely Brown

Beetle resisted the temptation to say that there was no need, as donkey had just completed the entire list. This was a time to provide his friend with empathy and support.

"But isn't it the case that you move from the stables to here every morning," beetle prodded the ground to define 'here', "are loaded up and walk from here to the mine and back, you then return to the stables every night?"

"Well I think you are minimising my efforts somewhat." donkey replied reproachfully. "As I've said I make four trips, sometimes five, who knows perhaps six before I return at night, each time carrying different things…"

Beetle's resolve faltered and he impatiently finished the description for donkey "... with assorted loads of food and tools."

"Yes assorted ... changing!" Donkey stressed the word 'changing' as beetle seemed to be having trouble making the connection himself.

"Changed" corrected beetle.

"Changed, changing what's the difference?"

"Well you aren't changing the loads, they are changed for you" explained beetle.

"Ok changed loads." Changed, changing, it's all the same thought donkey as a hoof again scraped the floor in frustration, this time a little more forcefully.

Beetle did his best to ignore what for him was a minor dust storm kicked up by donkey, as he added, "But every day is the same!"

My Job

"But I'm a donkey working in a mine, it's my job. I do have a job. I don't get to swan about all day like some," he said pointedly with beetle his clear target. "I have work to do," underlined donkey.

The perceived responsibilities of 'having a job' had been a topic of heated discussion between them on a number of previous occasions, a point not lost on either.

"You may have work, but it's the same each day. You don't even have to sort out your own accommodation, or food." Beetle realised he was reacting to the freshly fanned heat of their previous arguments. He instantly regretted mentioning the accommodation which was his usual riposte to donkey's 'I have to work' line of argument.

"The point is that each day is like the last and the next. That's not really dealing with change."

Beetle clearly wasn't understanding, so donkey decided on a new tack.

"You say I don't change, but I'm always on the move, I never rest. I'm not like, like…" Donkey searched for an illustration "… the mountain we're walking on. Now you can say that doesn't change, but me, I never stop!"

After a brief pause he added, "In fact I'd say I change more than you beetle, I cover miles every day."

Beetle didn't want to lose the moment by descending into a futile 'who covers the most ground' or even 'who has the longest legs' argument as had been the result of previous discussions on the fairness of their lives. He continued to explain the realities of donkey's situation as he saw them.

"You start at the stables, come to the supply base, then the mine, base then the mine; it's round in circles."

"Not circles!" Donkey reacted indignantly to the implication of the word circle.

"Well back and forth then, and then back to the stables."

Strangely donkey seemed contented with 'back and forth'.

Sleep

"I know, but that's where I like to sleep. I'm comfy at the stables, I like it there."

Donkey spoke with a level of feeling which reflected his belief that he was describing some fundamental inalienable law of the universe.

'Begin challenging your own assumptions. Your assumptions are your windows on the world. Scrub them off every once in awhile, or the light won't come in.' Alan Alda

"Fine, but tomorrow you will go back and do it again. You're a donkey but you're stuck in a groundhog day!"

Beetle hadn't meant it, but donkey felt victimised and indignant. He hung on tightly to his inalienable bedrock.

"Well we've all got to have somewhere to sleep! Sleep is important and I like to know where I'm going to be doing it. When I wake up I like to know what I'm going to see. It makes me feel comfortable, relaxed and ready to face all of the problems that the day is going to throw at me."

He paused absentmindedly for a moment, as if to immerse himself in the sensation of sleep, before adding,

"Sleep is the best part of my day, why if I could sleep from morning 'till dusk, I think that might just be the most perfect day I could imagine."

'Beetle muttered under his breath, "It's difficult to see how you could be more asleep than you already are donkey, plodding round in circles."

But what he said was, "I know it feels like change, but it's a strange kind of change without really progressing. All the time you are moving, but every day is just the same. Movement isn't always the same as change."

Goldfish

Beetle's concern for his friend was that if the mine closed, donkey's world, the world he knew, would be gone. He could sense that his argument was beginning to hit home, but wanted to pull short of hurting his friend's feelings. With that thought he set out to diffuse things a little.

'A great many people think they are thinking when they are merely rearranging their prejudices.'
William James

"It's like a goldfish I once got to know for a while. Well I got to know him, and he got to know me thousands and thousands of times."

Donkey smiled

"It was great at first. I'd go up to his bowl and he was just so pleased to have someone talk to him. Every time he'd tell me how no one ever talked to him, not a soul, left alone isolated and ignored. The first few times I tried to argue with him, told him that we'd talked before, but it was no use. Then I took to taking on a completely different identity each time we met. I'd be called José and speak in a Spanish accent, we'd start a conversation then he'd swim round the bowl and greet me again like a total stranger, so I'd be Olav and tell him of my time in the Polish Shipyards in Gdansk. Another orbit of the bowl and I regale him with tales of my time aboard ship plying the Pacific Ocean, or travelling to the poles as a stowaway in the rucksack of an Antarctic explorer. But there was no future in our friendship. I'd no more than set the scene for the story when he'd be introducing himself again and saying how no one ever talked to him, ever! At first the challenge of changing my identity, thinking up new characters was fun, but the conversations just couldn't go anywhere."

He shouldn't have, but he added, as he recalled the reason for the story coming to mind,

"You haven't got goldfish in your family somewhere have you?"

Awake

"Believe me, if he had I'd be able to smell it."

They each span around startled to face the owner of the voice. Cat had suddenly sprung to life. He had a habit of doing that. He'd be paying no attention at all, for all the world he appeared to be fast asleep, then he'd join in as if he'd been following the conversation all along. Then, just as you'd got used to him being there, he'd doze off again. They'd grown to expect it, but it still startled them when it happened.

Cat continued, "But you're right, those goldfish are just so plain gullible. You pounce on the bowl and spook them by trying to fish them out, and by the time they've swum around the bowl they're saying 'how do you do' and introducing themselves afresh."

He licked his lips mischievously as he added,

"I've got to admit that there's something I really like about their approach."

Cat stretched himself and set to cleaning a paw before asking,

"That reminds me, is it time for dinner yet?"

The remark passed almost unnoticed, beetle and donkey, through much practice having become deaf to cat's favourite line of questioning.

Having joined the conversation, cat was determined to continue with his insights without waiting for further invitation.

"I don't think donkey actually forgets, but he allows a kind of amnesia to descend. It's just plain easier not to worry about real change, and instead let yourself think that the work you do is change enough."

Cat switched paws for a little more cleaning and added,

"The way he sees it, there's enough work to do already without having to go inventing work, by changing everything all the time."

Donkey wasn't completely sure whether to be insulted or encouraged by cat's intervention, but quickly decided that this looked like a line of argument that he might like, and have the reassurance of support from cat. It would be good to feel supported, even though he doubted that cat knew the first thing about change. He continued to explore this train of thinking in his head. Yes he'd already dealt with as much change as anyone could reasonably be expected to, and more than most actually did, beetle and cat included. He couldn't be expected to deal with one single bit more.

Too Much

The situation having been clarified to his satisfaction, donkey continued with renewed confidence,

'It takes a lot of courage to release the familiar and seemingly secure, to embrace the new. But there is no real security in what is no longer meaningful. There is more security in the adventurous and exciting, for in movement there is life, and in change there is power.' Alan Cohen

"You see, I've got my work to do and when it's done I deserve my sleep, that's my reward for putting up with all that I have to. It's not easy hauling things all day, not over this terrain."

He prodded the ground unaware of accidentally sending another small dust cloud in the direction of beetle, before adding,

"There're traps all over the place, deep holes that could kill a lesser animal. I need my sleep to build my strength for climbing out of those holes. If I didn't get back to the comfort of my stable and have a good night's sleep, I might never have the strength for all that climbing. I might find myself in a hole I just can't escape from."

He turned to face beetle accusingly.

"It's all right for you. You don't fall like I do, you've got those extra legs, and you're not at the height that I am, and... and the holes don't trap you like they do me. When I fall I do it big style, so I need strength to haul myself back up."

Donkey stretched himself tall as he spoke to emphasise the act of climbing from holes.

"I'm not just the strongest of us three, I'm probably the strongest animal for miles around, and if I get my sleep there's no hole that I can't climb right out of. There's never been a hole yet anyway and I'm willing to wager there's never going to be."

"We'll let's hope you're right." said beetle conscious that his energy was flagging in the face of donkey's single minded defence. He felt sure that if donkey's approach was a little different, he'd avoid falling in the holes instead of spending his time climbing out of them. However donkey had become so accustomed to working this way, that if truth be told, he now actually thought that a key part of his job was to climb out of holes.

Donkey's growing confidence coincided with beetle's reticence as he sought to collect his strength. He glanced briefly in the direction of cat to check if he could count on his support, only to see that he had re-curled himself and gone back to sleep.

Changed

Donkey pressed on regardless.

"You say that I don't change beetle, but you're always doing the same thing; flitting here and there measuring, counting, checking and rechecking. Those antennae of yours never stop flicking and flicking. In fact that's all I ever see you do."

Donkey wiggled his ears and rolled his eyes in an imitation of what he saw as beetle's giddy behaviour as he continued.

"I might be falling down a hole, or climbing out of one, or plodding along, in fact you never know what I'll be doing from one moment to the next. But you, you're always touching and checking things whenever I look your way, you're even doing it now!" he added reproachfully.

Sure enough beetle's antennae were flicking to and fro, as they always did.

"... and you call me a goldfish. What's with this checking and rechecking? Do something different, change!"

Donkey's confidence reached a crescendo and he finished with a flourish.

"If it looks like a rock and feels like a rock, it's a rock! Believe me! Leave it alone and move on."

In his excitement, another stamping of the ground and ensuing dust cloud, this time accidentally fanned in beetle's direction by an exuberant swish of his tail.

Of course in a way donkey was perfectly correct. Beetle did incessantly flick his antennae and swivel his eyes, constantly searching, looking, sensing, checking and rechecking. This was what he did all of the time, unchangingly. But donkey was the kind of correct that was actually fundamentally incorrect, and his confidence would all too soon be sent crashing down.

Beetle, offended by this final attack, tried to contain his anger. He had tried to remain calm, tried to help, tried to let donkey discover how he misunderstood the challenge that he faced. And what did he get by way of thanks? His words came out singly as staccato blasts.

"What do you mean, that's… *all*… I… do?"

Donkey's line of thinking was cut short as beetle continued.

"Can't you see?"

He strained to regain his composure and moderate his tone as he explained.

"I constantly check so that change won't take me by surprise. You see me constantly asking questions, collecting information; yes I do that all the time. This is how I deal with change."

"That's what I said, you are always checking, so I'm right, you never change!" responded donkey, unintentionally signalling his total lack of comprehension.

Changing

Gradually recovering his calm, beetle began to elaborate.

"What you see me doing is dealing with change, but you don't see what I'm achieving. I'm always changing what I'm achieving, going down new routes, travelling new paths, but you don't notice that. What you see is my behaviour, the scurrying and twitching, the behaviour of dealing with change. It's so dominant and unswerving that you think I never change, but what I achieve is changing all the time."

Beetle looked into donkey's eyes for signs of comprehension, and continued despite their absence.

"Don't look for the evidence of change in what I do, but in what I am, what I've become. You say I'm always the same – you're right but don't confuse that with the absence of change, it's the presence of change. What you could say is 'he's always the same – he's always changing, he is change.'"

Donkey's puzzled expression showed no sign of lifting, but beetle continued animatedly to explain what he saw as a critical point. Standing on his two hind legs and pointing to himself with the other four in an attempt to underline 'being change', as he continued.

"Because I collect information, and evaluate and check, I see the first signs of change, the danger of a hole I might fall into, the opportunity for food at the merest indication. I spot the slightest shift in the terrain, or merest whiff of the scent of food on the air."

"But you don't have to deal with …" Donkey attempted to interrupt to explain the challenges he faced, but was cut short as beetle continued.

"You don't see me climbing out of holes I've fallen in to, or desperately turning the ground in the frantic search for food when hunger strikes, because I've sensed and dealt with these well in advance. My journey hasn't the drama of yours, and avoiding holes and finding food don't stand out as activities, because if I'm doing change correctly, being change, they aren't activities at all."

He sought to underline the point,

"Believe me they are critically important for me, just as they are for you, but I don't focus on them. My focus is on change; it's always on change."

Beetle had nipped donkey's argument in the bud and although he hadn't yet understood what this might mean, donkey had the unnerving feeling that his current understanding might be about to be turned upside down. He sensed that he needed more information and probed for it.

Becoming

"So it's like change is your number one priority, it's the thing you do before anything else?" Offered donkey tentatively.

"No. It's more than that, much more. It's my only priority."

Beetle drove home his point.

"When you see the twitching antennae and the scurrying, you see me and change together. I have been joined to change. I've become change."

Donkey felt the remnants of his understanding were ebbing away, but beetle stepped in to continue.

"I find that if I focus on change, then the holes, food and a hundred other critically important things are automatically taken care of. Achieving them becomes a side effect of dealing with change."

Then, almost as if he surprised himself by the revelation, he added,

"In fact I sometimes don't even realise how important something was, before I find that I've already dealt with it. My focus on change means that if it's important it makes its way up the list of priorities automatically, and just gets dealt with."

Perhaps it was the returning sense of insecurity, but the word 'priorities' seemed to strike straight back into the hurt that donkey felt about having to work.

"Yeah, well I have priorities too." he interrupted.

Imposed

"Yes but you allow your priorities to be forced on you. When you've fallen down a hole it kind of becomes a priority to climb right back out again."

"That's right." He said excitedly, mistakenly sensing that beetle perhaps understood the pressure of real work after all.

"But whose priority is that?"

"Well mine of course!" donkey's confidence was now returning.

"Yes but you didn't choose it, you had it thrust upon you."

Bliss! At last recognition that he alone had to work, he would savour this moment. He began to slowly and pointedly spell out the conclusion.

"Well we can't all decide how to spend our days you know. I have to work for a living. I have to haul things. There are things I have to do. I can't just decide how I'll spend my time."

But with lots more savouring left to do, donkey was interrupted as beetle continued unabated.

"Donkey! I have to work for a living too; we are both the same! We have to do whatever to get our food, secure our accommodation and the other things we need and want. It's exactly the same."

Donkey was desperate to tell beetle that his work was real work, important work and different. That beetle didn't understand. That what he hadn't taken into account were the special circumstances, the differences. Beetle sensed this and barely drew breath as he marched on.

Choice

"There is no difference. If you want to hide behind the fact that you don't have control, that you're special because you have to carry things, then don't kid yourself that you have no choice – that *is* your choice. If we choose to let

'In this theatre of man's life, it is reserved only for God and angels to be lookers-on.'
Pythagoras

someone else make the rules then it's still our choice whether we follow them or not. Our life is ours alone, no one else's no matter how much we may feel it to be."

Beetle paused but donkey no longer felt inclined to interrupt.

"We all have choices. Sometimes they're not easy ones to make, and we might find it easier to think that it's a choice that's already been made for us by someone else. That's never the case. We might allow ourselves to stand in line behind someone else making the decision, but when it comes to call, the decisions are always ours, whether we make them or not."

Me!

'Every job is a self-portrait of the person who did it. Autograph your work with excellence.'
Anon.

Donkey could see what beetle was saying and he agreed. He agreed in a general sense, it made sense, for everyone, everyone else, but he was different. Beetle didn't know about his situation.

It was true that beetle didn't know about donkey's particular situation, but he knew it was different, just as everyone else's situation was different; that's what made them the same. He knew the uniqueness that donkey was feeling and how this was standing in his way. He'd felt that uniqueness himself, just as everyone does. He tried to help donkey understand it.

"There's nothing wrong and everything right with hauling things if that's what you've decided to do. If that's your choice then it's as good a desire as being a soaring eagle or a dolphin arcing through the surf. The key is that it's your choice, and in choosing it you thereby choose to make it part of what you become, your life's work if that doesn't sound too grand."

As he said it, he felt 'life's work' sounded precisely too grand, and he quickly tried to explain.

"What I mean is it's not simply something you are doing. If it's just that then it's not really what you want to do. It has to be something that you are committed to doing well."

He paused for a moment, and then added.

"Deep down we all want what we do to matter, to the people around us, those we love, to ourselves so we feel we are growing, and to the people we leave behind, so it feels worthwhile that we were here."

Donkey felt he agreed, but something within him stopped him from agreeing. To buy time as he pondered what might be the reason, he ran his nose along the surface of the grass, as if searching for the perfect blade to eat.

Motive

Beetle wasn't to be distracted and took the chance to confront donkey's thinking,

"So donkey, have you chosen to work in the mine?"

His immediate reflex was to answer 'of course', but he felt the question burrowing to a deeper level, a level at which donkey hadn't asked that question of himself for a long, long time. In fact he couldn't recall exactly, or for that matter approximately, when it had last been asked.

"Let me help you. Are you just hauling stuff or ... are you part of a team working to get the Earth to give up its precious metals? Metals that will be turned into thousands of useful items that will transform folk's lives."

'If a man is called to be a street sweeper, he should sweep streets even as Michelangelo painted, or Beethoven played music, or Shakespeare wrote poetry. He should sweep streets so well that all the continued….

Beetle pressed donkey to respond, with exaggerated sweeps of his arms to stress the intentional grandeur in the phrasing of his question.

Donkey paused from his affected search amongst the grass. "Well I just haul food and tools up ..."

"... are you hauling stuff or part of a team that's achieving?" Beetle pressed again for an answer

... continued hosts of heaven and earth will pause to say, here lived a great street sweeper who did his job well.'
Martin Luther King

"Does it matter?" replied donkey in exasperation. He didn't like the thinking he was being forced into. It was like a stick disturbing the long settled mud at the bottom of a pond.

"It matters a lot! Listen to yourself. When you talk about hauling stuff you keep saying 'just', 'just hauling'. 'Just' doesn't sound like something you've chosen for your life. It sounds like something that you are making do with, something that lets you cope. Are you just coping or living?"

Beetle was determined to stir that mud.

"I'm living of course!" Donkey cried indignantly.

"Well why are you just hauling stuff then?" With this he gave the stick one last spin.

"I'm not just hauling, I'm... I'm... I'm making a difference. Without me it wouldn't happen, the mine wouldn't be working."

"So?"

"So I am part of the team that's achieving!"

Donkey resented being forced into an answer, but as he heard himself say it he recognised that he had genuinely never thought about his work this way before. He did his work. He did it as well as he could. He was conscientious and he didn't think he moaned much, but he hadn't thought about really choosing this to be what he did. I guess he felt that he'd kind of arrived at doing this work; kind of stumbled upon it. He'd arrived at a point on a journey without being able to recall the steps he'd taken to get there, or whether he'd ever really planned that this was a point he intended to reach. It wasn't that he'd felt he begrudged the work or even really disliked it. But he'd never before felt that he'd actually chosen it.

Freedom

His anger at the stirred mud was being replaced with a new and unexpectedly strange feeling.

"I chose to work here."

He felt good that he'd discovered that he was doing what he wanted, but he felt better than that. No he felt good for a deeper reason. He felt good that he was now aware of being able to choose what he was doing. He felt strangely more in control of things. If he had chosen that this was what he wanted to do, then he had control over how he did it, control he'd never really seen or felt before.

'Nothing splendid has ever been achieved except by those who dared believe that something inside of them was superior to circumstance.' Bruce Barton.

Strangely although this control, and sense of wanting to do the work, seemed to bind him more closely to the mine, he also felt much more freedom. He wasn't sure quite where this freedom came from until he heard beetle next speak.

Beetle had watched for several minutes as donkey had contemplated his discovery before saying,

"That's right, you chose to work here."

"Yes … yes I did, and if I chose this as what I want to do, then I can choose something else."

He thought for a moment and concluded with a smile

"I'm free to choose something else."

This explained the freedom he felt.

Beetle joined in energetically to add fuel to this fire,

"It's more freedom even than that."

He waited until donkey's eyes focused on his own before adding,

"Every day you *have* to choose. You must decide, is this what I choose to do today? If it is then I commit myself to it. It's what I have chosen. If not then I start to move to find out what it is I do choose to do."

Beetle stressed the idea of choosing as if the word itself had its own intoxication.

'There is a great deal of difference between the eager man who wants to read a book, and the tired man who wants a book to read.'
G.K. Chesterton

Donkey's reflection on this need to choose was cut short as beetle continued.

Magic

"I know that you've cursed me donkey because you are forever having to climb back out of holes, whilst I never seem to have to. You call it luck or blame me having more legs, or even think I have a sixth sense. Can you believe it? A sixth sense! Have you seen the size of me? I hardly have room for the first five!"

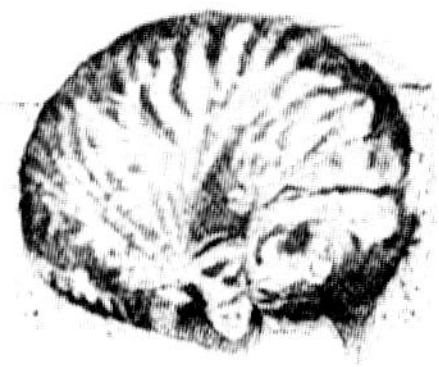

Before continuing he looked up to see donkey smile, and from the corner of his eye he noted cat, still asleep yet with his paw flicking across his face to ward off the attention of a large unwieldy fly.

"I don't achieve things by accident, luck or magic, by sixth sense or even my sixth leg. Just because I'm not climbing out of holes doesn't mean I'm not doing what's required to avoid them, and just because I'm not digging for food, doesn't mean I'm not doing what's required to stave off hunger. If the fact that I don't make a song and dance of it, don't huff and puff in getting things done, and don't complain about my bad fortune makes it seem to happen like magic, believe me it certainly isn't..."

With a final flick of the paw, the fly was sent spiralling, and departed in a dizzy zigzag trajectory away from cat.

"... The things you spend your time battling with, fighting to achieve and grumbling about are not my focus. Not because they're not important, but simply because I don't let them become my focus. If I did that, then I'd be constantly switching from searching for food, avoiding the holes, getting some sleep, searching for food, avoiding holes and so on. I'd always be working on one thing and worrying that I'm not doing the others. I'd be going back and forth..."

"...or round in circles." donkey interjected. He was beginning to form a new understanding, though it took beetle a couple of moments to acknowledge this as he continued.

"As for a sixth sense, when I concentrate on change I find the five senses are more than enough!"

Beetle paused sensing that his point had at least begun to be made. They each stood for a few moments absorbing what had been shared and maybe a little of what had not.

Indirect

The sun passed behind one of the small puffy clouds which now dotted the sky. Its shadow briefly revealed their world painted with a new palette of colours. The change prompted donkey to speak first. He felt his old understanding had been undermined, but was unsure about what might fit in its place. He began tentatively.

"So what you're saying is that I have to do things at the same time, think of things all together."

He sensed that this couldn't be right, but was unsure why. He found himself thinking aloud.

"Well it's difficult enough to concentrate on one thing at a time." He added as the thoughts crowded in, "You might say I have choices but that's not how it feels. I've got deadlines, things to deliver, schedules, consignments. If I was thinking about food and sleep at the same time, I'd never get anything done."

Something was wrong, either in the argument or his understanding. He suspected the latter.

Beetle could see donkey's painful struggle as he tried to create space for his new understanding.

"No it's not a case of thinking of things together," said beetle, "That's kind of what happens, but that's not the route to it. The secret of thinking change, of becoming change is not to approach it directly."

As donkey had suspected, it was the latter indeed. He didn't need to speak. His puzzled expression was a more than sufficient cue to beetle.

"Well it's a strange thing that change happens most often when you aren't trying to force it." Beetle's voice reflected a hint of intrigue with the idea.

"So change happens when you don't try to change?" Donkey paused for a moment. "Well I guess I'm vindicated. If I'm not trying to change, I must be trying to change!"

Flock

Beetle recognised that in a real sense donkey had captured the paradoxical nature at the heart of change, and of its understanding. He knew that this was a paradox that served to lock the door to real understanding for most folk.

"Let me try to explain."

Beetle was keen to seize the moment and help his friend unlock this door. He looked beyond donkey into the distance to see the dappled green fields of the valley below.

'How wonderful that we have met with a paradox. Now we have some hope of making progress.'
Niels Bohr

"Now you've seen the sheep in the bottom field?"

Beetle knew that donkey had whiled away many an hour, watching the shepherd at work on the farm in the valley near his stables.

"Yes of course. Those sheep, they stand around all day eating grass. Now if you want an example of lack of change…"

"… and the shepherd trying to round them up?" interrupted beetle keen to continue for fear that his thought might drift from his mind.

"Of course, the shepherd and the sheepdog." Donkey wasn't sure where this was leading, but it felt good to be back on familiar territory.

"Now when he's trying to gather the sheep together, the shepherd opens the gate to the pen and what happens?"

Donkey thought for a moment.

"Well nothing. The sheep just ignore him and carry on eating grass. Nothing happens at all."

"And then?"

"Well he starts to whistle, but the sheep pay no attention, just more munching."

"And?"

"Well then the dog chases them into the pen!" donkey said triumphantly.

"Well sort of, but how?"

Donkey was worried that the questions had been so easy to answer, and fearing some trap, quietly adds the footnote,

"By sneaking around the sheep?"

"Absolutely!"

There was no trap!

"And what would happen if the dog chased straight at the sheep?" continued beetle.

"Oh that's easy, they'd just run away."

"Sure, they'd scatter. So he moves around, not chasing but encouraging. The shepherd opens the pen, and the dog encourages them to go in that direction."

Donkey paused for a moment whilst he connected his string of responses, joining the dots to arrive at a conclusion.

Relaxed

"I see. It's not as if the dog forces them into the pen. It's the sheep that go in by themselves. They decide to enter the pen."

"That's right."

"The dog just encourages them to choose to."

"That's it exactly," confirmed beetle. "In a way that's how change is. You can't force it because you can't know what lies ahead in the future, or is around the next corner. And often if you try to force things they just become more and more jammed or run off in the wrong direction. You have to create the right conditions for the change to happen."

"The open pen?"

"Yes, and encourage the change."

Donkey scratched a hoof along the ground, and a small clutch of pebbles slipped into the channel he created.

"So, you approach change, without really approaching it."

"Yes. It sounds strange, but you know it's happening not by the banging of drums and the commotion of dealing with change; it's actually the opposite. Things are relaxed, there's no panic, no frenzy, and the uneducated..."

"... might mistakenly think there is no change," interrupted donkey.

'If you seek, how is that different from pursuing sound and form? If you don't seek, how are you different from earth, wood or stone? You must seek without seeking.'
Wu-Men

"Yes, but this is real change; a lack of drama and things appearing to happen by magic, luck or a sixth sense."

Donkey looked down the mountain and into the distance to see the sheepdog at work. He looked through eyes with a faintly superimposed mind's eye picture of a new image of change; a fragile image that almost immediately began to slowly fade.

"I think I see what you mean about not forcing change, just encouraging it to happen. And I can see the sheepdog dealing with things together. But with sheep it's easy - that's how they behave – all together."

Donkey was struggling to relate this simple picture to his own circumstance. "I have different priorities that pull me in different directions. It's impossible for me to work on them all at the same time."

Priorities

'You must understand that seeing is believing, but also know that believing is seeing.' Denis Waitley

"But donkey, isn't it just the same with sheep. You've already said that if the dog ran at them they'd pull him in just as many different directions."

"I know I did."

Donkey had said it and believed it and felt uncomfortable at how easily his argument had been undermined, but still sought to deny his admission,

"But it's different with sheep. I have to deal with different things at the same time."

Attempting to bolster the frailty he recognised in his argument he added,

"The sheepdog just deals with sheep. I don't have a choice. I have to deal with things one at a time; the sheepdog doesn't have to."

He was frustrated and acutely aware of how poorly this reflected the utter impossibility he felt in tackling all of his multifarious tasks simultaneously.

"You're right that the sheepdog doesn't work on things one at a time, ignoring the rest whilst he concentrates on getting each one into the pen. But it's the way in which he deals with them together that holds the secret."

Beetle pointed in the direction of the sheep as he explained.

"Look. We can see he doesn't deal with them one at a time. But if we look closely, he also doesn't try to manage the flock as fifty individual sheep, each needing to be encouraged at the same time on their own individual routes to the pen. If a single task of encouraging one of the sheep is challenging, then fifty tasks in parallel will be impossibly difficult."

Donkey pondered. He agreed that fifty tasks would be fifty times more difficult than one task, probably more so, and this was at the heart of the discomfort he felt. But this appeared to be exactly what the sheepdog did.

"But he does deal with the sheep all together. Doesn't he?"

"Well that's how it appears, but that's not what's really happening" replied beetle. "He deals with fifty things, by doing, not the old thing fifty times over, but by doing one new thing."

"A new thing? What's this new thing?" asked donkey scarcely concealing the hint of desperation in his voice.

"He doesn't deal with fifty separate challenges, he deals with them collectively by dealing with change, change taking place in the flock."

Beetle could see that donkey was struggling to grasp this distinction, and began to elaborate.

"You've watched the dog at work. What happens if a sheep moves a little distance away from the flock?"

Using his newly acquired vocabulary, donkey replies,

'To develop a complete mind – study the science of art; the art of science; learn how to 'see'; realize that everything connects to everything else.' Leonardo Da Vinci

"The dog encourages it to move back."

"That's right. It automatically becomes a priority. Not by being lost and needing a special search. Not because it is that sheep's turn to be dealt with. But by being just a little further out than the rest. And as soon as it's back in place it's no longer the focus of attention. Another takes its place for a short while whilst it's the farthest from the flock, then another and so on."

Donkey nodded silently in agreement as beetle continued.

"There's no great fuss about this prioritisation, it just happens quietly and automatically as the dog deals with the changing situation."

Seeing

Beetle allowed donkey a few moments to compare the picture that has been described, with his own experience of watching the sheepdog at work. Once he is contented that donkey sees no conflict in the description, he adds,

"If you think about it, the dog doesn't deal with sheep at all. He deals with the changing shape of the flock. If he does that, then the sheep will take care of themselves. You see, the secret is that the sheep aren't the dog's priority, change is. In fact the dog no longer sees the sheep, but just the change in the shape of the flock."

For a moment donkey toyed with this description of an activity he'd watched, perhaps hundreds of times. As he did, a new picture snapped into focus. He saw a new understanding emerge from what had been merely the shadows of what he'd previously seen.

'The changing flock, that's it!' thought donkey. 'He no longer sees the sheep, just the flock, just change.'

Like a shaft of light this thought illuminated his understanding. The sheepdog hadn't mastered the task so well that it could be done fifty times over; no this was something new.

He raised his head high and made several large swishes of his tail, as if energised by this new thought.

"I see. It's a new way of seeing; the dog sees the change in the flock, not the sheep."

This was the something new, and it had been right under his nose all along. 'The dog has change as his priority, not the sheep' donkey said to himself several times over. He wanted to hold onto that image. He'd watched the shepherd and the dog many times; he'd watched but hadn't seen. The next time he *would* see. At least one part of a new understanding was in place.

'Everything is connected... no one thing can change by itself.'
Paul Hawken

He didn't speak as he contented himself by playing in his minds-eye a movie of the sheepdog at work and making sure that his new understanding was secure. This is what he had to capture. However vivid, he knew it could disappear soon, leaving him grasping at thin air.

Beetle left donkey to ponder his thoughts and set to mapping the contours of a nearby stone with the tips of his antennae. He clambered over its surface, examining small fissures and indentations, feeling the texture and testing its earthy smell.

Meanwhile donkey continued to replay his mind's eye movie, stretching the envelope of his understanding. With difficulty he tried to extend it, to see this new way of seeing applied to other situations, his situations.

A butterfly caught his eye as it perched on the purple ball shaped flower head of a clover, its proboscis probing deep into the blossom. The clover swayed slightly as the butterfly clung on tightly, fanned by the gentle breeze donkey had until that moment been unaware of.

'I see the butterfly, I think I see it, but what am I not seeing?' he thought to himself. 'How could he see what he couldn't see? Or even know when he wasn't seeing?'

He turned over this question several times, yet each time seemed to reinforce the apparent impossibility of the challenge. It seemed he understood perfectly the picture painted by beetle, but as soon as he tried to frame that picture around himself, he found the perfection disappeared, leaving him grasping at shadows.

"I understand, but as soon as I try to think what it means to me, it all starts to disappear." Donkey paused for a moment before continuing to outline his discomfort.

"You say I have to think about change by not thinking about change. But if I'm not going to think about it, when do I start not thinking, and isn't that what I'm doing already before I ever knew there was anything to think about, or not think about?"

His spirit followed the downward spiral of his words, draining both his understanding and his energy. The swish of his tale was this time in frustration as he added.

"Now I thought I really understood, but it's all getting confusing again."

Becoming

Beetle could feel the turmoil in donkey's thinking and the paradox at its heart.

"It's the way you think about change that needs to change," beetle offered.

Donkey looked up as beetle continued. "When you said that the sheepdog had a new way of seeing, you were partly correct. It's actually a new way of thinking. He thinks about the challenge of rounding up the sheep in a totally new way."

Donkey tried hard to concentrate as he listened to beetle's explanation.

"He thinks not in terms of what he has to do, but what he must become."

Already donkey begins to feel unsure. "Ok, but what does that mean. I am only what I do. If I keep doing the same things then I won't change."

'The greatest discovery of my generation is that human beings can alter their lives by altering their attitudes of mind.'
William James

"But the magic of being indirect isn't reached through what you do. Think about it, if change were something you have to do differently, you'd just tell me that you haven't the time and your day is already busy with work from dawn till dusk."

"I would, and it is," confirmed donkey obligingly.

"When you think that way, you wait for the perfect moment for change. This is where most folk go wrong. The time for that perfect moment always stays out of reach, locked in tomorrow. There is no right moment. You aren't waiting for a special time or for things to line up in a special way – you are waiting for 'you' to be ready. That can happen anytime or never. Again it's up to you."

"Up to me?"

'Take the risk of winning.'
Frank Dick,

Donkey felt the shift in responsibility as a shiver down his spine.

"Yes. Most folk are so scared of that idea that they never let that time arrive. They keep themselves busy, fill their time up with things to do, convince themselves they're dealing with change..."

The familiarity of this description was not lost on donkey.

"... but the instant they are ready, then everything *is* changed."

Donkey noted the stress beetle placed on the change being instantaneous. Not 'will change', but 'is changed'. It didn't make him feel comfortable at all.

'Before enlightenment I chopped wood and carried water.
After enlightenment I chopped wood and carried water.'
Zen Saying

Beetle continued,

"The things you do might look just the same, but the thinking, the reasoning, in fact the person behind them, will all be different."

Donkey continued to toy with this notion of the immediacy of change. He tossed the thought around his head, vaguely aware that this was important, but not sure why, as he listened to beetle expand his explanation.

"Sheepdogs are successful, not because they can do fifty tasks in parallel, but because they don't think sheep anymore. They connect with and become part of the change."

Paradigm

"So it's about me being ready to change?"

Donkey had an image in mind that kind of made sense, but felt as fragile as the clouds floating above them.

Beetle nodded.

'All things change, nothing is extinguished. There is nothing in the whole world which is permanent. Everything flows onward; all things are brought into being with a changing nature; the ages themselves glide by in constant movement.'
Ovid

"So it's about a frame of mind, my frame of mind?" added donkey.

Donkey wasn't quite sure what this would mean to him. It felt as if he were stepping from the firm ground of what he thought he had known, and out into – what, he didn't quite know.

"If that's the name you choose to give it, yes," replied beetle.

"So I have to change my frame of mind?" Donkey pondered whether the task of change had suddenly become very easy, or very difficult as he asked the question.

Beetle perhaps sensed this as he replied.

"Yes, but just as with rounding up the sheep, the way to change your thinking is not directly by forcing it, but by enabling, creating the right environment, the space for it to happen."

Donkey was still distractedly struggling to determine whether the task had become simplistically easy, or impossibly difficult. He chewed on a clump of grass, hoping this might help.

"All effective change is about enabling, creating space," beetle continued. "And the first place you need that space is in your own thinking. You can't expect the things you do to reflect the real spirit of change, if your thinking isn't enabled first."

This made a kind of sense to donkey. It was the sort of sense that things with a top a middle and a bottom make. But what the whole amounted to, he wasn't at all sure, and he felt a little fearful of finding out.

Beetle climbed to sit atop a smooth flat sand coloured pebble before he pressed on gently, leading donkey into what he knew would be a completely new type of difficult terrain.

"Imagine a sheepdog who's thinking that he rules the field and the sheep just better obey his every word. He's stronger than they are, he's the boss and he's sure that he's cleverer than them."

Donkey pushed the nagging question of whether change had become easy or impossible to one side, as he tried to imagine just such a sheepdog, as beetle continued.

"If that's his mindset, he's going to charge straight in there barking his orders and no matter how fierce he is, or how right he is in thinking that the sheep need to go into the pen, it won't make a jot of difference. There'll be sheep running and bleating and jumping over fences and pretty soon scattered to the four corners of the farm."

He saw donkey give a nod of confirmation before adding,

"The dog's got to first change its thinking, from trying to direct change, to enabling it."

'Learning is a willingness to let one's ability and attitude change in response to new ideas, information and experiences.' Peter Vaill

'So it isn't just a new way of seeing, it's a new way of thinking', donkey thought to himself as his understanding began to take a new shape. But he still couldn't imagine how this new thinking emerged through what the sheepdog does, and found himself asking.

"Yes but what does he do to enable the sheep, to encourage them into the pen?"

Having stepped off the solid ground of his old understanding, donkey was keen to grasp at anything that felt solid.

Learning

"Now at first he might not know how to enable the sheep to get into the pen," beetle continued. "He's never done that before, but his new thinking will start to help him. Instead of thinking he has the answers, he starts with questions. That's the first part of his new thinking."

"So he doesn't know...?" was donkey's almost startled response.

It wasn't put so much as a question, more the involuntary expression of the fact that he hadn't previously contemplated 'not knowing' as a possible start point.

"Of course not, at first. It's the first time he's tried," confirmed beetle. "Instead of 'I know', 'I'm the boss', he starts to ask 'how could I come to know a little more?'. 'What could I try and how might I learn from it?'"

"He's got to find out?"

"Sure... So he might try a little bark and he sees what the effect is. Maybe the sheep run away a little. Then he tries a growl. He tries moving left and then right. If you look at him, his ears are pricked up and his eyes are keen."

Beetle holds two claws to the top of his head to imitate the pricked ears and swivels his eyes scanning his imaginary flock, as he continues.

"He's looking for the slightest clues to tell him what the reaction has been. He's looking at the sheep and looking for how they are behaving. When do they move and when do they stop? What makes them settle back to eating grass and what catches their attention?"

"Yes I've seen him doing that, concentrating hard on what the sheep are doing," confirmed donkey.

Beetle continues in an almost conspiratorial tone as he now reveals the secret of the dog's ability.

"What he's doing, is learning."

Before continuing he pauses and notes the signs of recognition in donkey's eyes as he savours the significance of the idea.

"He's trying different things, watching the reaction, and understanding what went on. With this learning he starts to change what he's doing. He barks a little louder in some situations and sits a little quieter in others, refining what he does from what he's learned."

Beetle looks straight into donkey's eyes to underline the mystical force of what he then reveals,

"Then something magical happens, a transformation…"

Donkey is hooked, waiting for the secret to be revealed, his ears focused to pick up beetle's next words.

"… the sheepdog's actions are no longer his own. Oh his aim remains the same, of getting the sheep into the pen, but instead of going at it directly, he has become responsive to the situation."

He pauses momentarily before underlining the magic of the transformation,

"If you ask him what move he'll make next, he probably can't tell you, because it's no longer up to him."

"It's not?" Donkey senses the magic.

"No. His next move is determined by the flock, by the change going on around him. He's no longer working to a fixed plan to achieve his aim, but an agile one which will change to meet the changing challenge that he faces."

Letting Go

With the unique feeling of dawning understanding, donkey adds quietly,

'The world is ruled by letting things take their course. It cannot be ruled by interfering.'
Lau Tzu

"He's taken control by letting go."

Beetle smiles and allows donkey to savour the joy of his own learning. He scuttles around a small area, examining his surroundings, a small crack in the earth and the fallen head of a flower. His antennae twitching, checking and rechecking, leaving donkey to a few moments thought.

After a minute or so donkey adds,

"So change is his priority, and learning is his priority?"

His statement is phrased with the hint of a question.

"That's it. You've learned a lot already. They are both his priority because change and learning are the same thing, real change that is."

"The same thing?" donkey says wistfully as he thinks of the two ideas, change and learning.

"Yes, once change ceases to be your plan of what you are going to do; the big sheepdog setting out to bark out his commands. It becomes the responsive way in which you enable change, automatically responding sensitively to what's happening around you and learning. It becomes what you are being. When this happens, then you see that learning and change are ways of looking at the same thing."

'Change and learning' donkey thinks to himself. "That's perfect!" He reflects for a moment before continuing. "They are the same thing, you're right. You can't know what the sheep will do next, it's just not possible, so you can't have a fixed plan of what to do. Change has to be based on what you are learning."

"And the ability to change, based on what you are being," adds beetle.

Donkey played the two words 'change and learn' over in his mind. It was as if an archaeologist faced with a thousand fragments of pottery before them, had suddenly pieced together two parts which met precisely and revealed the previously invisible beauty of a long lost vase. The words fitted together so perfectly that he marvelled at and played with their connection. He couldn't help but describe to himself his discovery of seeing these two ideas, in a completely new and now connected way.

'Learn to pause.... Or nothing worthwhile will catch up to you.'
Doug King

"Change *is* learning and learning *is* change."

The confrontational and competitive nature of their earlier exchanges, each striving to make their case, had been replaced. Now there was less talking and more thinking, reflecting, imagining.

Donkey was beginning to enjoy this new thinking. Now he had begun to grasp it, it seemed less of a threat.

It had felt a frightening and unfathomable extra task, a task he could well avoid. But now it had the feel of opening doors, of creating opportunities. He wasn't at all sure how or why, but inescapably he was excited by the thoughts.

How?

Again he had the feeling that this new understanding had to be captured, secured for fear that it might disappear like the melting snow in spring. He had the image of change being indirect, something you do without setting out directly to do it. He smiled to himself that whilst he could see the inherent contradiction, he now understood well what this meant.

He began to chew at an appetising clump of grass, trying to savour his new understanding, but struggling to quiet the voice within him. Life had trained him to think in terms of things to do, and this kept returning to his mind and threatening to dissolve his understanding. After all, he thought, the sheepdog has to do something.

'We shall not grow wiser before we learn that much that we have done was very foolish.'
F. A. Hayek

Beetle could sense the churning of this thought in donkey's mind,

"What is it?"

Donkey tried desperately to disguise his 'what does he actually do?' question as he sensed that although it rang persistently in his head, it was an old question, part of his old thinking and one that he knew should be replaced, but he did not yet know with what. Failing to reconcile the problem he finds himself blurting out,

"That sounds difficult for the sheepdog," and immediately wonders why those particular words found their way onto his lips and adds "Well, learning how to encourage the sheep; which bark to use, which movement causes which reaction, that kind of thing."

Donkey's question tails off to a whisper as his insecurity is revealed. He is not hopeful of the response.

Can't Know

"That's the easy stuff!"

Beetle's answer confirms a sense of deep foreboding for donkey, as he wonders whether he may have completely missed the point.

A feeble "eh?" is all he can muster, but fortunately beetle isn't looking for a response and presses on to explain.

"What's there to be learned is easy. The really difficult thing is allowing yourself to learn. I mean really learn."

Donkey need not have worried about the quality of his question. It's clear that beetle has given much thought to this and is keen to share his understanding.

'The way I see it,
you can either run
from it,
or learn from it.'
Rafikki to Simba
in Disney's The
Lion King

"In order to learn, first you have to accept that you don't know. That's hard for some folk, just too hard for many. It's what people sometimes call ego, having to admit to others, and more importantly to yourself, that you don't know."

Donkey thinks that maybe the snow is safe for the moment. There are lots of things he doesn't know, and things he can't do, and it's never been a real problem admitting it.

"First?" asks donkey.

"Sorry?"

"You said the first thing was to accept you didn't know," he feels better for having helped beetle continue the description.

"Oh yes, beyond that you have to admit that you never can know, that's the killer blow for most folk."

'Question everything. Learn something. Answer nothing.' Euripides

Donkey contemplates this additional information. He strains to think of things that he will never know. It seems far easier to list the few things he will ever know. He is still pondering when beetle comes to his aid by adding more.

"Not everyone has this ego thing ..."

'That explains it' thinks donkey comfortingly.

"... but for those that do, it's difficult to accept you can never know. You see, whatever you learn only reflects what happened so far. For the sheepdog, all sheep won't be the same and tomorrow you might meet one who behaves completely differently to your experience. If you've got ego and find it hard to learn, that comes as a hammer blow, a personal affront. You see it as failure, not as the chance to learn more."

Beetle eases forwards as if to confide another secret, as he continues half whispering.

"You see it's not a case of working out the answer once and for all of how you shepherd sheep. becoming an expert and qualified."

He shakes his head, antennae swishing to and fro, as he adds,

"Oh no, it's a case of accepting that you've got to go on learning for ever. You are always going to be taught a lesson, and sometimes when you least expect it."

In a whisper that donkey strains to hear he adds.

"Imagine the sheepdog that thinks he rules the sheep..., when all along it's the sheep that he has to learn from. Imagine how that would feel if you had ego."

The conspiratorial tone of the delivery serves to underline the gravity of the revelation.

"Oh I see, it's the sheep who are teaching the sheepdog!" summarised donkey.

A grin spreads over donkey's face at this realisation, "I can see how this ego thing would really mess that up."

He imagines the sheepdog in the bottom field, thinking he's been watching him control the sheep, when all along he's been learning from them, and adds, "So you have to be prepared to learn, to accept that you don't know."

Practice

Donkey felt relieved. So there are things that you can do, but they are things to change your thinking, your way of thinking. That was what he had been missing, a connection between doing things differently and thinking differently. He reflected, "Change and learning really are the same thing." And just to check his understanding he asked,

"So change and learning are about starting with no knowledge, and building it all up from scratch?"

"Well yes and no."

Donkey smiled that whilst he hadn't known how beetle would reply, he had started to expect his questions to solicit an ambiguous response. It felt to him to be the nature of this indirect enabling, of achieving change by not setting out directly to do so, and to live with this ambiguity was in the nature of living with change. He was starting to know what he didn't know, and for the first time was able to appreciate that this represented progress.

'Alice: Nobody ever tells us to study the right things we do. We're only supposed to learn from the wrong things. But we are permitted to study the right things other people do. And sometimes we're even told to copy them. ...continued.

Beetle continued,

"It doesn't pay to start everything from scratch like the goldfish or there's a danger that you never progress anywhere, you just keep repeating the same thing over and over again."

"That's what I thought. Surely it's best to learn from others?"

...continued.
Mad Hatter:
That's cheating!
Alice: You're quite right Mr Hatter. I do live in a topsy-turvy world.
It seems like I have to do something wrong first, in order to learn from what not to do. And then, by not doing what I'm not supposed to do, perhaps I'll be right. But I'd rather be right first time, wouldn't you?'
Lewis Caroll

"That's true, but you have to take care to avoid one of the biggest hidden dangers of change."

"Dangers?"

"It's possible to learn from others, but only if the thinking is right. Remember it's the thinking that has changed in the sheepdog."

"I see, but?" It was clear that donkey didn't see at all, as beetle continued.

"The thinking has to be of change and learning. This doesn't mean you *can't* learn from others, but you have to be really careful that it's real learning."

"Real learning?" donkey questioned, unaware that there was any other kind.

"It's another example of being indirect," explained beetle. "Unfortunately lots of folk think they are learning when they find out what others do. They think they learn by taking what they've seen and applying it. But often they haven't learned, they've just collected something new to do."

"What? The thing they thought was good wasn't?"

"Maybe it was, but that's not really the issue. They are looking for a shortcut, but the real shortcut they take, is to short-circuit their thinking and learning. They mimic what they've found without really understanding how and why and when it works."

'They know enough who know how to learn.'
Henry B. Adams

"So they just copy what they've seen working?" asked donkey somewhat puzzled. He allowed his mind to wander a little as he nibbled a small but juicy clump of grass. After a few moments of unsuccessfully trying to uncover the flaw in the idea of copying, donkey adds, "But isn't that ok?"

He'd been struggling to think of learning as anything other than copying what you saw or were told to do. It seemed that everything he'd learned from his handler had been just that way, by being told or shown.

Questions

"Well it could be, but it's the way you arrive at it that's important."

"Indirectly?" Asked Donkey, correctly guessing at the approach needed, without really understanding what it might mean.

Beetle explored the smooth inside of a fallen acorn cup, perfectly shaped to that of the acorn it once held, as he replied.

"Rather than something to do, when you look at the way someone else does something, see that as an opportunity to learn. See it as something you could try in your situation and learn what the results are for you."

His antennae seemed magnetically drawn to the smoothness of the cup's inner surface as he continued. "The big problem is when you take something that has worked for someone else and use it just because it worked for them. This is just crazy."

Donkey's nod reflects the conviction he felt beetle express, rather than any conviction of his own, as beetle continues.

"They used it in a different place and different circumstances and …" beetle seeks to underline his thoughts, "… in a world that no longer exists."

Beetle rolls over the acorn cup with his forelegs and examines its contrasting gnarled exterior.

"Wow! A world that no longer exists?" donkey echoes.

Beetle looks up from his examination, a little startled at donkey's response, "Well a time that no longer exists if you prefer."

"No!"

Donkey didn't say so, but 'a world that no longer exists' felt absolutely fine. He wasn't questioning it, just revelling in the idea of a new world existing, just because time had passed and change had happened. Like the cloud moving from in front of the sun, lifting the shadow and revealing fresh new colours. He liked the thoughts that idea brought. He liked them a lot.

Beetle continued,

"If you take what someone else has done, think of it as a suggestion of something you might try, but with no view of whether it will work or not, until you try it yourself in your circumstances and learn."

There was that word 'learn' again, donkey thought as he replied.

'A good question is never answered. It is not a bolt to be tightened into place but a seed to be planted and to bear more seed toward the hope of greening the landscape of idea.'
John Anthony Ciardi

"So don't presume that it will work"

"Or even that it won't work. This way you can even find things that didn't work for anyone else but suit your circumstances and work for you."

"So it's a thought of something you might try?" checks donkey.

"Yes exactly, but you've got to be ready to learn, knowing that you don't know"

"Yes I see. So not assuming it works, or doesn't"

"Even more than that. Try not to even think of answers; working or not working. Think of questions instead. Tell yourself that a good thing to do doesn't exist; it can't exist on its own. It only exists when it sits in the right situation to make it good, or bad, and even on this little mountain that's changing all the time. So there aren't any answers, not ones that stand still long enough to be used, only questions."

Donkey spent a minute or two thinking about worlds that no longer exist, as he chewed on another clump of fresh grass.

"I guess this grass will no longer exist in a few minutes, and tomorrow and each day this will be a completely new field."

Beetle nodded.

'You can become blind by seeing each day as a similar one. Each day is a different one, each day brings a miracle of its own. It's just a matter of paying attention to this miracle.'
Paulo Coelho

Every day he ate the grass, and every day the field was full of fresh grass, so it made perfect sense and the evidence was all around him. However donkey couldn't recall ever entering the field and seeing it as brand new. Now he knew it to be the case, he pondered why.

"That's right a new field every day, and no reason why tomorrow it should look like today." added beetle, unheard by donkey as he continued to wonder at whether he'd be seeing the field as fresh and new, or through fresh new eyes.

'Maybe it's both', he mused. 'If the field can be new each day, then why can't I' he said to himself.

Donkey continued devouring the grass and as he allowed his mind to wander, a stream of images conjured by what they'd discussed crossed his mind. The sequence finally settled on that of the sheepdog, an image that was familiar, yet new. By the time he'd devoured the clump he was working on, he was ready with a new question.

"So do the sheepdogs learn from each other?" he asked.

'Give a man a fish and you feed him for a day. Teach him to fish and you feed him for a life.'
Chinese Proverb

Beetle replied from the summit of a smooth sided pebble, the latest target for his impulsive and inquisitive exploration.

"Oh yes. The shepherds have sheepdog competitions where all the dogs meet and share their best practice."

"I've heard the dogs mention the competitions," confirmed donkey.

Beetle once more adopted a conspiratorial stance as he spoke.

"The secret is they've learned not to share what to do, barking, running, chasing and the like. They all live on separate farms, in different locations, different terrain, and of course different sheep."

"I see?"

"Sharing what they do might give them something to try but isn't the real value. No they mainly share how to learn, how to listen, how to observe, how to understand, how to question, how to measure. What they share is how to get better at learning."

"Better at learning?" echoed beetle, his response has less the sound of a question, rather that of a door to his understanding beginning to open.

"That's what's of value to them and of value to the rest of us too. I've learned a good few things about learning from the sheepdogs, and I'm never going to round up a flock of sheep, that's for sure."

Beetle pauses whilst his antennae explore the exposed roots of a tree poking up through the surface of the ground. Several seconds pass before he becomes aware of the silence. He looks up to see an expression of complete concentration on donkey's face.

After a few moments donkey nods and says "So even the learning is indirect."

"What?" replies beetle a little puzzled.

"Well the learning is learning to learn." He can't suppress a smile as beetle congratulates him.

Illusion

"You've travelled a long way whilst standing in this field my friend. Yes learning to learn, I like that."

"Learning to learn." Beetle repeats as he rolls over a small pebble examining its underside, and then adds, "The dogs actually hold a competition for who brings the best practice at 'learning to learn' as you call it. The winner gets to win the sheepdog competition."

It takes a moment for the significance to hit donkey, "You mean ..?"

"Oh yes! The shepherds think it's a competition between them to determine who is best at penning the sheep, but the result is worked out by the dogs beforehand, based on the sharing of learning."

"And the sheep?"

"Oh the sheep are in on it of course, it wouldn't work without their agreement."

"So the sheep decide whether to go in the pen or not according to who's meant to win?" asked donkey.

"Well as you now know, they decide to go into the pen anyway, so they just make sure that no one gets giddy and runs into the pen too soon and spoils the result."

"So it's not the shepherds at all?"

Donkey enjoys savouring the feeling of discovery, a sense of special knowledge.

Beetle breaks off from his latest investigation to reply.

"Heavens no! In fact the shepherds haven't really understood this enabling thing at all. They think that they are instructing the dog with all the whistling and gesturing that they do."

Donkey smiles, recalling some of the antics that he's seen the shepherds getting up to, leaping and cavorting around, whistling and waving their arms and using a stick to try to guide the sheep.

"Of course the dogs don't let on," beetle continues, "they follow the instructions, to keep the shepherds happy, but not so far as to allow the chaos that would take place if they followed them directly. No they play along, but at the right moment they drop a shoulder, make a quiet growl or whatever's needed to keep things on track."

Beetle chuckles to himself as he adds,

"I wouldn't like to imagine the chaos if the dogs were to let the shepherds loose on their own. It's the dogs that understand real change and ensure that things are relaxed and unruffled. That is unless the shepherd panics and starts whistling and shouting and scaring the sheep."

Both beetle and donkey relax as they savour what they've learned. Beetle reflects for a minute or two as his antennae explore the surface of an intriguingly misshapen pebble before adding,

"It's lucky for shepherds that dogs have a soft spot for people."

Donkey smiles and chews on another clump of sweet tasting grass as he muses to himself, 'All that time watching the sheep and never seeing what was really there.'

'You do not pull out a radish to see if it is growing well.'
Peter Senge

They each quietly go about their tasks. Beetle exploring nothing yet everything, and donkey with heightened senses in search of the perfect morsel of grass. After a few moments beetle adds,

"It's a funny thing those shepherds not understanding enabling. They only have to look at the crops in the field to see that you have to provide the right situation, the climate and soil conditions, to enable them to grow. You can't force them."

"Just provide the right conditions" echoes donkey. "And then stand back."

"That's right. And that standing back can sometimes be the hardest part."

Opportunity

Donkey continues to chew at the grass with a growing sense of contentment. He likes this feeling, a feeling of expanding his understanding. It's not a feeling he is used to. He recalls that in his early life whilst being trained, he was made to wear blinkers on his eyes to focus his attention on the steps ahead. Trained not to look to the side, not to see what beetle calls opportunity. Though his eyes have been free of them for many years, he's now aware of those on his thinking, and is happy to feel their grip loosening a little.

Somehow the grass seems to smell and taste a little sweeter, no he concludes that its taste is perfect. He savours its perfection as he lets new thoughts percolate through his mind, and with it sudden realisation.

"So now I understand why all the scurrying around, and the thing with the twitching antennae. You are learning just like the sheepdog."

"With my antennae I'm constantly collecting information, building a picture, checking and rechecking. Even if I've found something like a rock nearby, I keep going back to check that it's still there, or to find out what's changed. This way I keep learning and building up my knowledge of what I've encountered, so I can sense change and deal with change, not rocks and holes that take me by surprise and become a priority. The more I learn the more I know, and the better I can avoid problems and exploit opportunities."

Donkey feels an embarrassing sense of chagrin as he recollects his previous outburst.

"Oh, I'm sorry about the rock thing earlier."

"Oh that's ok. If it feels like a rock and looks like a rock, it usually is a rock… except of course for when it isn't," chuckles beetle.

"So you can always sense things that are changing, and never hit problems?"

"No I didn't say that. Just like there's a lot of different sheep, there's a lot of world out there to learn about, and it just keeps changing. But each time I make a mistake it's just like finding something new, so I add it to my understanding. Like you said, every day it's a new field, even if it looks like it did yesterday, it's still new. So you can't know for sure what's going to happen. You have to be prepared to try things and to learn. You might begin by trying something that worked in the past, so long as you're not expecting it to work this time."

"You're hoping it will?" Asked donkey.

"Oh sure you'll be hoping it will, but also be ready for the world to have changed so it doesn't. If you're in a learning frame of mind, it kind of doesn't matter whether it works or not."

"But you want things to go well?"

'I have learned silence from the talkative, toleration from the intolerant, kindness from the unkind; yet strangely I am ungrateful to these teachers.'
Kahil Gibran

"Of course, but sometimes things going well, well you reach it..."

"Indirectly!" Donkey correctly guesses.

"That's right."

"So making mistakes is ok?"

"Well you might call them mistakes, but you're kind of in that answer way of thinking where things are right or wrong. You're back to being the sheepdog whose sure they know best. If you're in the questioning frame of mind, then if things don't turn out how you thought they would, you've just created something to learn from."

"I guess so, but a mistake's a mistake, right," replies donkey.

"Well yes and no. Actually, looking back, some of the best things to happen have come from things that didn't work out how I expected. I mean sometimes straight away they just turn out better than what you intended, but more often the learning leads to something good further down the road, something that you wouldn't have had otherwise."

"Really?"

Ideas

Beetle spends a few moment contemplating past experience before adding,

"When something goes completely right, you maybe don't know quite how it worked. Maybe it was skill, perhaps luck played a part, but you just can't be sure. So when you come to try it again, all you can do is to try and repeat what you did. Maybe the luck or circumstances you are relying on just aren't there. But if you've in a learning frame of mind then you're ready to try things and find out more about why. "

Donkey's head is buzzing with ideas in a way that he can't remember it ever buzzing before. He feels more strongly this sense of freedom.

The blinkers are off so he can see options and opportunities and can try new things. He can choose, and even if he gets things wrong, he will be learning and learning to learn. He wants to learn more, about mistakes, learning and people. What has beetle learned from people, he wonders. His head is filled with a hundred questions, but before he can ask he is interrupted from an unexpected quarter. Cat has stirred again.

Awareness

"I like what you're saying about change beetle, but don't go giving too much credit to those dogs. They get just too close to people for my comfort. There's such a thing as maintaining your cool."

Cat licks his paw, runs it through the fur on his head and combs back his ears as he continues.

"All that waiting at the window, barking and wagging their tail when their people come home, it's just not dignified."

"Have you been listening all along?" asks donkey, "We thought you were asleep as usual."

"Asleep or awake, I'm always listening," replies cat.

They let this comment pass, as they let much of cat's intermittent contributions pass, but would soon learn that this was a significant and important truth for cat. Had he known it, donkey would have recognised this as an insight into cat's unsuspected capabilities for change, and would not have said what he was about to say. However, flushed with the feeling of his newly elevated status in such matters, donkey boldly asks,

"And what could you possibly know about change cat?"

Treating the comment with a disdainful elegant slow stretch, cat eventually replies,

"We cats are the grand masters of change."

Agility

Donkey scarcely contains a burst of laughter as he replies.

"I know beetle talked of change being un-dramatic, but surely you don't think that dozing under a bush all day qualifies you as a change expert. I mean there's indirect and in-direct."

Donkey could no longer suppress his laughter, but it was quickly muffled when he saw beetle's furrowed brow.

"Donkey, have you learned nothing from beetle here?" asked cat pointing at the smallest of the trio.

Donkey felt the newly acquired mantle of 'change expert' begin to waver as cat continued.

"When it comes to learning and being change, beetle may have understood the theory, but we cats have taken it to a new level. It's not just our thinking that has 'become change'. With us cats it's the whole deal – we've truly totally become change."

Cat paused to allow the full import of his announcement to be felt. Donkey didn't know what was coming, but began to expect ,what he was determined now to call yet another learning opportunity.

"We cats have mastered change so well that you can hardly see the effort we put into it. Just like you and beetle, we've got important things to tend to."

Prompted by a thought flashing across his mind, cat adds,

"We didn't eat yet did we?"

Cat seems always ready to eat, so both donkey and beetle have become accustomed to the question, and their practiced response of gently shaking their heads.

"No. Ok. Anyway where was I, oh yes important things. Now beetle explained how effort isn't consumed in chasing after one thing and then the next. Beetle's sense what's happening, they see the signs and just glide into what's needed."

Sameness

Another pause. This time cat struts a little with his tail raised high, before continuing.

"Anyway beetle's got himself so relaxed and into change that things happen kind of automatically, and that's good. But even beetle would admit that all that twitching and scurrying around just isn't cool. It's effective I'll grant you, but cool, no way."

Donkey saw beetle nodding in agreement. He was undeniably impressed by cat's statesmanlike performance, and fascinated at the prospect of what he was going to say next. It had crossed his mind that beetle's scurrying looked awfully tiring, but this was one of hundreds of questions bubbling in his newly energised brain, that he'd not yet had chance to voice.

"Well we cats have moved beyond that. Instead of having to check and recheck to see what's changed since we last looked, we've really committed ourselves to change being our only priority."

"What, by going to sleep?" interjected donkey, inappropriately tapping into the residue of newly found confidence.

"Going to sleep? Well in a way I guess it might look that way," replied cat. "Kind of like only being awake to change."

Cat hadn't thought of it that way before, but liked the idea prompted by donkey's question.

It was clear however that donkey's prompting had been somewhat unwitting as he questioned, "Awake to change?"

"That's right." Cat paused to think before adding, "Actually we've developed our senses so change is the only thing we see."

"What do you mean – only thing you see?"

Fascinated though he was, donkey still struggled to see the slightest shred of evidence of cat's claimed Grand Master status.

"Well we cats decided that sameness just didn't matter enough to take notice of. Sameness just isn't where it's happening."

Cat could scarcely contain a purr of satisfaction at the phrase and replayed it to himself ' ...just isn't where it's happening'.

The satisfaction is cat's alone, and passes seemingly unnoticed by donkey.

"We only want to know about change. It's kind of like if a scene isn't changing, we sort of don't see it after a while, or if a noise is constant, we don't hear it."

"Seems kind of weird!" replied donkey shaking his head. "Does this happen with all your senses?" he adds a little intrigued.

Perception

"Well nearly, it also works with smell and touch."

"And taste?"

"We've not perfected that one yet. It's a shame because I'd love to try asparagus tips and pickled onions, we all would, but we're still irresistibly drawn towards tuna and chicken. Still four out of five isn't bad, and there's a cat saying says we should always have something to strive for."

Cat smiled and purred to himself at the delivery of an in-joke for grand masters of change, though it meant nothing at all to donkey or beetle.

'If we are lucky, we can give in and rest without feeling guilty. We can stop doing and concentrate on being.'
Kathleen Norris.

"So how do these senses, the four that don't see sameness, how do they work… or not work?" asked donkey who couldn't help but think that cat might just be afflicted with a peculiar kind of disability.

"Well let's imagine that I'm looking at something; a nice fluffy rug in front of a large crackling log fire, the kind I love to curl up next to."

Cat paused and his eyes began to flicker dreamily as he conjures up the scene. The pause becomes prolonged as the dream grows ever more lucid.

"Yes and…" interrupts donkey with sufficient force to break through cat's trance like state.

"Well if I'm there looking at the rug, after a few minutes it kind of fades away."

Donkey hesitates for a moment waiting for more; the words that would bring sense to cat's explanation, but none are forthcoming. Finally with no little sense of exasperation he probes,

"And that's it! That's your approach to change? Why, that's just you falling asleep in front of the fire. We can all do that! It hardly qualifies you as a change expert!"

"Well of course it could be," replies cat, "And falling asleep is certainly part of it, but that's not what I mean. Let's imagine that on the rug is a nice juicy mouse, the kind I like to ..." Cat's eyes began to roll with the thought.

"Yes we herbivores get the picture," beetle and donkey chorus.

"Well imagine the mouse stays perfectly still."

"Not a good plan I wouldn't have thought, but do go on," nudges donkey.

"Well that's the funny thing. If it stays still, the mouse and the rug just fade away, even if I'm hungry and feeling like ..."

"Even if you're hungry?" asks donkey incredulously.

"Yep."

Bingo!

"And then what?"

"And then what – nothing," replies cat.

Donkey nods with raised eyebrows desperate to encourage cat beyond the 'nothing'.

Another nod and cat accepts the prompt. "But if the mouse moves, then it's action stations, everything kicks in and bingo!"

"Bingo indeed!" donkey concludes, as cat demonstrates graphically the actions that bingo encompasses, finishing with a lick of his lips.

"Yes all automatically" cat continues, "just like beetle was explaining. And it doesn't just happen with mice. Dangle a little toy on a string, or jiggle a piece of thread and its bingo again. Before I know it I've reacted and pounced."

Cat considered the mesmerising effect of a dangled thread, before adding, "Sometimes it's so quick that even I can't tell whether the thread moved first or whether I just knew it was going to."

To donkey's ears this was indeed the revelation of yet more magic.

"And it's the same with the other senses?"

"Yes the slightest noise that's different and my ears spin round to locate and identify it, and if it's a mousey noise …"

"… then bingo!" adds donkey denying cat the opportunity for further graphic details.

Dreams

"And this works all the time?

"All the time." confirmed cat.

Donkey begins to piece together the evidence,

'Awaken your sense, your intuition, your desires. Awaken the parts of yourself that have been sleeping. Life is a dream, and to live it, your must be awake.'
Rachel Snyder

"I see, so when you are sleeping, you aren't sleeping. That's how you followed our conversation?"

"Oh no, when we are sleeping we're sleeping alright, because there really isn't anything better to do when there's no change going on. Sleep is the place for dreams. But as soon as there's change, then the alarm goes off and it's action stations."

"So your number one priority, even above sleeping, even while you are sleeping, is change."

Cat nods and donkey thinks through the wonderful implications of what had been described. He shares his conclusions.

"Now you truly are the grand master. Sleep is my favourite thing, I'd do it all day if I could, and you, well you can. You can sleep but not be gone. That is truly impressive," donkey adds wistfully, clearly taken aback by what he has learned.

Enjoying the palpable admiration that he has generated, cat continues his description,

"It's surprising how much spare time you have when you deal with change effectively, and sleeping is my favourite way of spending that time."

'Doing nothing is better than being busy doing nothing.'
Lao-tzu

It was clear that sleep held at least as much attraction for cat as it did for donkey, whose inadvertent sighs seconded cat's every word.

"Of course before we worked this all out, we cats were haring all over the place chasing after everything, running after every noise, scratching at everything we saw."

Cat scanned around to check that they weren't being overheard before continuing,

"Have you ever seen dogs chasing cars?"

Both confessed that they had.

"Well that how we were – though don't go telling dogs that I said so. Of course it wasn't all bad; it's how we became so fit and agile, but we were exhausted most of the time and not the least bit cool! We slept a lot then too, but it was a different kind of sleep. But once we had it sussed there was no turning back."

"And who was it that sorted it out?" enquired beetle.

"Oh now you're asking. That goes back a long, long way. The story goes that it was some cats from out east somewhere. Apparently they were some seriously cool characters."

"Persian cats?" offered donkey not knowing quite where the suggestion came from.

"You heard that too!"

'I was born not knowing and have had only a little time to change that here and there.' Richard Feynman.

Cat was seriously surprised that such inside information had been leaked, and so badly that even donkey was aware of it. "I never really knew whether those stories were true or just fable, but I guess ..." Cat resolved to look into this a little deeper later with his cat friends.

Donkey had much thinking to do. He churned over this new learning in his mind. So that was cat's secret. Now it all made sense. He'd never understood the way cat just jumped in and out of conversations. The way he seemed to sleep so much. Yet he always had whatever he needed, indeed so much that he could afford to be choosy. He seemed always to land on his feet. Donkey smiled to himself at the thought that figuratively and physically cat always lands on his feet. Whatever he needs just seems to be there when he needs it, even the ground when he falls.

He thought of the last thing cat had said about the thread '*...can't tell whether the thread moved first or whether I just knew it was going to...*' this was indeed the stuff of magic.

Not Knowing

The more he considered it, the more overwhelming the evidence appeared for cat's grand master status. How could he not have seen the signs before? He felt a cold shiver run down his spine. He'd accused cat of knowing nothing about change, yet he'd become change. It was clear that it was he who failed to understand.

His mind slipped back to the discussion of not knowing. What was clear was that this willingness to accept that you don't know, and can't know, was not only critical to becoming change, but was much more difficult than he'd imagined. Even for donkey who didn't think he had this thing beetle called ego, it was easy to forget that you didn't really know anything.

'Confidence, like art, never comes from having all the answers; it comes from being open to all the questions.'
Earl Gray Stevens

The questions now bubbling in the newly heated cauldron of donkey's head would have to wait as he was cast into a new shadow.

"Come on boy, let's be off with you."

It was donkey's handler coming to collect him and lead him back down to the stables, his day's work done. Beetle shouted a farewell as donkey was led off with cat running alongside, his tail held high and rubbing his body against the handler's leg. Cat's elegant dancing between the handler's strides calculated to encourage the delivery of a tasty titbit.

Their discussions would have to wait a while, but donkey strode with new purpose and saw the route back to the stables through new eyes, keen to sense and learn. Beetle felt that donkey had learned much and knew that he too had learned about the nature of learning and change. He looked forward to helping his friend grow further as he set off in the direction of his accommodation along his regular, though intentionally unfamiliar route.

The Second Day

Contemplation As was often the case on the mountain, the weather turned and the next two days were cloudy and wet. A ferocious wind drove the rain into every crevice of the mountain's rock face.

'It is one of the most beautiful compensations of this life that no man can sincerely try to help another without helping himself.'
Ralph Waldo Emerson

Donkey was kept under cover in between his trips carrying supplies, and had little opportunity to see the others except briefly to shout a quick hello.

Cat seemed to spend the two days keeping dry and warm and as usual relaxed, and beetle was largely occupied with problems waterproofing his accommodation.

Donkey had much time to think. His mindset had begun to be changed. During the discussions he had felt the cracks appear in his old thinking. Some pieces had even fallen away. In their place were one or two new pieces. Roughly shaped and ill fitting, but new pieces all the same; exciting shiny new pieces. He had questions, hundreds of questions, things he didn't know, things he wanted to know, and at the same time he knew that with change he could never know. He'd liked the sense of holding and understanding these contradictions and paradoxes. He'd felt some, and was sure that there would be many more. Indeed he'd decided that paradox was key. If you don't feel the ambiguity, then you probably aren't experiencing change, aren't becoming change.

All of this had felt like a warm fresh bedding of straw. It had felt like his thinking had found a new home, a new place to live and grow. That's how it had felt as the discussion had ended, charged and enabled. But two days had now passed. He wanted to feel that same fresh thinking, but as he had feared, his snow had begun to melt, and now he struggled to recall its message.

Reversal

Although he was finding it hard to hang on to his new thoughts, but as his old ones returned he didn't feel the security that they had once provided. Instead he felt only their inadequacy, their falseness. The snow of new thinking was disappearing, but the old ground this revealed had even less substance than the fragile snow. He felt doubt and discomfort. Perhaps he had simply misunderstood it all. It was clear he had once known nothing, when he thought he knew all. He'd thought that he'd since learned, but maybe not. Wasn't it clear that beetle knew so much more, and cat unimaginably more even than beetle.

His thoughts swirled. He'd learned, but now it was all going, all gone. He hadn't learned at all. He couldn't learn. There was nothing to learn. He was donkey, a good worker, trusted, dependable, and capable. He worked well and would be respected and valued for working well. He had to concentrate on doing well what he did. That was his future. He knew what needed doing and each day he would do his work. He'd be roused from the stables and taken to the supply base. From there he'd take supplies, food and tools, up to the mine. Then he'd return and take more supplies, food and tools, up to the mine.... His heart sank as he found himself saying the words '... round and round in circles!'

This felt so much worse than before he'd ever talked with beetle and cat. Why couldn't they have just left him alone? He'd been happy, just doing his job, grumbling a little, but plodding along. It had felt right then. Everything had seemed to fit together. Now nothing seemed to fit.

He had been happy in the past, or so he thought, but it hadn't felt anything like he felt during their discussion. Then he'd felt energised and excited, capable and alive. This was happiness multiplied many fold. What had happened to that feeling? How had it seeped away?

The energy had begun to drain that first night, and by the morning it had all but gone. For these two days, donkey had plodded about his work, even more ploddingly than usual. He paid even less attention than normal to what he was doing, and really couldn't understand why he was doing it at all. He'd lost his old understanding, the old ground, and the new ground with it. He was bitterly unhappy.

Ready

On the third day the world at least returned to normal, even if donkey couldn't. The sun shone from another blue sky and soon the flowers and animals had dried out, and the rain was reduced to no more than reason to appreciate the sun.

Unusually it was barely the afternoon before donkey had been returned to the field alongside the supply base. His handler had been intending to take him straight back down to the stables. Donkey had been so listless and out of sorts that his handler was sure that he was suffering some sort of sickness. He'd decided to let him rest in the field before taking him down the mountain, and in the meantime set off to contact the vet to arrange for donkey to be examined. Donkey was oblivious to all of this. He'd been so distracted that he had no idea he'd only made three trips.

He hadn't been in the field for long when cat emerged from the long grass. He stretched and scratched at the ground before walking towards donkey. Beetle had hitched a ride on cat's back.

"Did you see that rain? Did you see it?" asked beetle before jumping down from his perch. "You don't know how lucky you are having your accommodations provided for you donkey."

As soon as he'd said it, he realised that he shouldn't have, and waited for donkey's retort. But there was no reaction at all from his friend.

Beetle looked at him closely.

"What's the matter friend, you got a bug?"

He chuckled, grateful that he'd been able to share one of his favourite beetle in-jokes. That it meant little to either donkey or cat made its delivery none the less enjoyable.

"Aw nothing" replied donkey without enthusiasm as he scratched the ground with a hoof, carving a neat furrow into the soft damp earth.

"Come on, you can tell us folk, we're friends," said beetle for both of them. Cat was already distractedly cleaning himself, running licked paws over his ears, doubtless in preparation for some sleep.

Donkey continued to scuff the ground as he replied falteringly, "It's just …"

"Yes?"

"Well …" Donkey hesitated, reluctant to give voice to his feelings.

Beetle watched his friend struggle for a few moments before offering his own description.

"It's just you're feeling unsure and detached, kind of lost a little, set adrift," he said as if reading from a menu of symptoms.

"Yes, set adrift and detached." replied donkey, selecting from the list.

He wonders for a moment how beetle could have known, but quickly dismisses the thought and continues.

"I liked our discussion but it's just kind of gone. I seem to have, - to have lost it."

Donkey's voice tails off to a whisper, reflecting the deflation he feels.

"Well that's good!" replied beetle with a level of animation that catches donkey unawares.

"Good?" Donkey pauses from his hoof scratching and looks up ready to berate beetle for his thoughtless sarcasm.

"Sure thing. That shows that you are ready for change." explains beetle in a matter of fact tone which serves only to amplify donkey's astonishment.

'We have to believe that a creative being lives within ourselves, whether we like it or not, and that we must get out of its way, for it will give us no peace until we do.'
Mary Richards

"Ready for change?" replied a puzzled donkey.

Although this sounded a lot more attractive to donkey than 'kind of lost', it most of all felt wildly inappropriate. He couldn't imagine feeling less ready.

"Yes sure." replied beetle whilst distractedly examining a small group of stones, in search of the driest place to rest whilst he caught the warmth of the sun.

Donkey was far from sure. He wasn't at all convinced that beetle wasn't about to play some hurtful trick on him, stringing him along before pointing out what he knew to be his abject failure.'

Having settled on a spot which met his needs, beetle continued gently, "Remember when we talked about the changes having to start with your thinking?"

Suspecting a trap, donkey hesitantly confirms his recollection, He was sure that he remembered something about thinking.

"And we said what you had to do," continued beetle.

Donkey could definitely remember something being said, but just what it was he couldn't seem to recall.

"... when we talked about the sheepdog?" offered beetle attempting to kick start donkey's memory.

Uncertainties

Words and images flashed across donkey's mind, sheepdog, yes, sheep, pens, shepherds, chasing, whistles, flock, priorities. He felt it was all in there, but he couldn't make sense of it, and the more he tried the more jumbled it appeared.

Beetle tried to help untangle the thread,

"Remember? The sheepdog has to begin asking questions instead of thinking he has the answers."

"Yes that was it, questions not answers," thought donkey, a light beginning to dispel the shadows as the picture formed in his mind, but still too indistinct to recognise.

"Well that's what you're doing. You are asking yourself questions."

Beetle's antennae begin to scan the next stone, checking that his is still the driest.

"Umm..." Donkey wasn't sure. Not sure at all. It seemed to him that he just felt lost. Nothing more, or less. Just lost.

Taking his prompt from donkey's obvious lack of conviction, beetle continued.

'It may be hard for an egg to turn into a bird: it would be a jolly sight harder for it to learn to fly while remaining an egg. We are like eggs at present. And you cannot go on indefinitely being just an ordinary, decent egg. We must be hatched or go bad.' C. S. Lewis

"You've probably got hundreds of questions in there to ask us and everyone else," beetle adds pointing to donkey's head. "But as we said, all change starts with the thinking, your thinking. And the first questions are questions about yourself."

Donkey scratched the ground again, but now with purpose, the scratching mirroring the energy of his thinking as he tried to decipher beetle's words. This was certainly starting to sound a little better. In a confused jumbled sort of way, perhaps that's what he had been doing. They hadn't felt as well shaped as questions, more anxieties, fears, discomforts, concerns. But maybe these were the sometimes distant relatives of questions.

Still unsure he examined beetle for some sign that he was being teased, and saw none. Perhaps that was it. Perhaps he had been asking questions. He just hadn't been able to recognise them as questions. But if that's what he'd been doing, then why did it feel so bad? Before he could pursue this thought, beetle continued.

"Now imagine the alternative."

Beetle prompted him to think, but donkey's mind was in no mood to cooperate, still struggling distractedly to piece together the contradiction it saw. After a few moments beetle prompted him again,

"The alternative - to questions?"

"The alternative to questions?" Donkey echoed confused.

"Imagine instead of being filled with these questions, these uncertainties and fears, you had been filled with certainties. Would that have been better?"

Donkey thought for a moment 'better yes, he wanted better' and was about to offer a tentative 'yes', but was soon glad he hadn't.

Paradox

"Of course not! The only certainties you can have are old ones, the old picture of the old world. That's the only place for certainties. No if you hadn't been full of concerns you wouldn't be ready, not ready for change."

Beetle continued to underline the point.

"Change is about weaving your way forwards through the uncertainties, not holding on to old certainties, or even replacing them with new ones."

The words 'weaving your way' latched in donkey's mind's eye. He saw an image of picking his way across the familiar pock marked surface of the mountain, the routes he had to negotiate every day. But this was slowly replaced by a brightly lit picture he didn't recognise. At first, he was blinded by a dazzling pure white light ahead of him. His feet became cold, then began to move and slip as the ground beneath them struggled to support his weight. As his eyes became accustomed to the new environment, he could just discern a barren white landscape of broken floating ice stretching to the horizon in every direction. He was trying to select a path that would bear his weight and lead him forwards. With each footstep the ice would move, sometimes a little, sometimes with loud and frightening cracking sounds, leaving his hooves in the icy cold. Wherever he stood to contemplate the next step, he could feel the ice creaking under his weight and the need to move onwards. The frighteningly vivid image stayed with him for a few seconds before slowly beginning to fade.

He moved a few small steps forwards to feel the reassurance of grass and earth beneath his hooves, only now he could feel the Earth itself straining beneath his weight.

"So if I'd felt that things were ok, that's the sure sign that they aren't?" Donkey looked for and received a nod of confirmation from beetle. It was another one of those paradoxes. He expected them and he'd told himself to be on the lookout for them, and here he'd missed a big one, a blindingly obvious one. Had he learned something, or nothing at all?

'Laugh at yourself, but don't ever aim your doubt at yourself. Be bold. When you embark for strange places, don't leave any of yourself safely on shore. Have the nerve to go into unexplored territory.'
Alan Alda

He spied a tempting patch of grass a short distance away and moved forwards slightly to more easily reach it, mindful of where he placed his hooves and the work of the Earth in supporting him.

Beetle took the opportunity to check out the ground around his latest chosen perch, antennae flicking, whilst donkey munched the grass deep in reflective thought. It was cat who spoke next.

"Now don't go beating yourself up because you didn't realise this, or you're back where you started."

Cat detected recognition in donkey's eyes and continued,

"When you start to get this change thing, you realise that this is what it's like. You don't have to get upset because you don't know. The fact that you know you don't know, means you are starting to know."

Beetle's brow furrowed for a moment whilst he replayed cat's words in slow time to check his understanding.

Donkey needed a moment longer to do the same. How did cat know that's what he was about to do, to start the cycle again of being annoyed because he hadn't known? And if it's about not knowing, how had cat known that's what he was about to do? 'I guess it's just that magic with the thread again,' donkey allowed himself to conclude, deciding that more thinking time wouldn't help unravel yet another paradox.

Cat continued,

"This stuff isn't easy. It isn't going to happen in an afternoon. It's not going to happen with a big bang. It's going to happen slowly and quietly."

"Stuff? You mean change?" checked donkey.

"Yes. To begin with, no one will know it's started to happen except you. In fact for most folk, they may first notice the opposite, they might think you're going backwards. So don't let them put you off. Soon enough those that know about change will know that it's started."

Donkey thought about how he'd been behaving for the past couple of days and reflected,

'One does not discover new lands without consenting to lose sight of the shore for a very long time.'
André Gide

"It feels like I've been going backwards"

"That's the feeling of movement. It feels kind of spooky at first, and it'll take a while to get used to it. Don't worry, forwards, backwards, it doesn't really matter, you're moving. Like a ship that's been locked in the ice, you're starting to break free." said beetle.

For a moment donkey wondered if beetle had read his mind's eye picture of creaking ice, or perhaps he really had travelled to the poles in the rucksack of an Antarctic explorer.

If he felt it as movement, then of course it made sense. It would take time to get the hang of it and move forwards, but he was moving, definitely moving. He had to remember this, burn the image into his mind so he could see this as progress, and not a source of anger. It was the feeling of beginning to change, beginning learning, beginning learning how to learn.

No Return

He could accept that he was learning, but this feeling of not knowing was much more frightening than he'd ever imagined. When they'd first talked he hadn't seen it as a problem at all. He'd been thinking that admitting a few more things that he didn't know would be easy. He realised now that what he'd actually been thinking was that he already knew what was important; had a pretty complete set of things he needed to know, so could manage with some others he confessed to not knowing. But that wasn't what it meant at all. It meant admitting that he didn't know anything.

He recalled beetle's words about the difficulty of learning, '…you have to admit that you don't know.' How right he was. Admitting to yourself that you don't know, not simple things, but difficult things, not unimportant things, but the most important things.'

Donkey takes a moment to spell it out to himself 'not knowing the most important things about yourself' and found himself echoing the phrase 'about yourself'.

Now that he understood, he couldn't think of anything more difficult. And what had beetle then said. '... the killer for most folk is that you never can know.'

Donkey stopped turning the words over in his mind, at least he tried to stop them, he tried to stop thinking, he didn't want to think, he couldn't stop, 'can't know the most important things about yourself, can never know ...'

Beetle who had been watching said quietly,

"This isn't easy... but do you remember how you felt the other day?"

Donkey couldn't remember anything, not who he was, where he was, who beetle was. He'd tried to stop thinking, but his thinking had gone into overdrive.

"I can't do this, I can't. Why didn't you leave me where I was?"

Beetle repeated his question,

"Do you remember how you felt the other day? When we talked about the sheepdog, the learning, choosing, options, do you remember?"

Donkey nodded hesitantly.

"That feeling is why this is worthwhile. Remember that, hold on to that. This isn't easy, but it's not just worthwhile, it's essential. You are ready to change, and therefore everything is already changed. There is no going back now."

"Yes but I can't do it. It's too difficult. I thought I was starting to learn, but you know so much more than me. I'll never know. I know you've said I'll never know, but you know so much. It's just too difficult."

Then beetle's words struck home; 'there's no going back now'.

Donkey felt panic flash through his body, "I just can't do it - be it! I can't be change, I just can't."

Movement

Cat dug his claws deep into the ground and executed an elegant stretch, unhurriedly arching his body to energise every muscle before offering his support.

"Don't worry friend. It's not about what you know, it's about what you will learn, and you've started to learn plenty."

Another stretch, this time with an exaggerated yawn completed cat's warm up exercises as he continued,

"Let me tell you something about people. Now people know plenty. They have special places where they go just for learning, and they don't just go there for a little while. Year after year after year they go, kind of filling themselves up with knowing. By the time they finish they are just like big buckets full of knowledge, and that's the point."

Donkey was shaken from his mental paralysis as cat's words began to conjure up new images. But almost immediately both he and beetle were taken aback as cat sat down having apparently concluded his contribution. He returned to his cleaning chores oblivious to the interlude his input had provoked.

"Cat?" beetle said quizzically, "perhaps for donkey's benefit, if you could just expand on your point."

"Oh for sure. Well the point is that they're finished, finished getting knowledge."

Before another pause could fully develop, beetle offered a helpfully nudging "And?"

"And?" replied cat as the prompt took a moment to take effect, before he continued,

"Well imagine this bucket being filled with knowledge."

Cat scratched the shape of a bucket onto a bare patch of earth, involuntarily releasing the characteristic smell of damp soil.

'Courage doesn't always roar. Sometimes courage is the little voice at the end of the day that says I'll try again tomorrow.' Mary Anne Radmacher

"It's a well used bucket so it leaks a little, not so much, but a little. We might call that leak forgetting."

He added a string of dashes to represent the drops leaking from the bucket.

"It doesn't really matter whilst the bucket's being filled, a little drip leaking away. But when this learning ends, when the bucket stops being filled, the leak is a little more important."

More dashes are added as his description continues.

"Then they grow a little older, the leak gets a little bigger. The bucket begins to empty, and the people start to notice. What do you think they do?"

Donkey, mesmerised by the image of leaky buckets, is too slow to offer an answer before cat moves on.

"Well I'll tell you what I would do. I'd open the tap and pour in some fresh learning, but that's not what people do. No they start to try and plug up the holes. Instead of getting new learning they hang on to what they know. They even fight each other for it rather than getting some new."

"They do?" asks donkey.

"Oh sure they do" continues cat. "They are so busy trying to plug those leaks that they block all the holes including the one at the top they filled the bucket through in the first place."

Cat hastily adds a lid to the bucket to underline his point.

"Now, if instead they just opened up that tap and started refilling, they might find that the new knowledge tastes a lot sweeter than some of the old stuff. They might even find that they'd like to open up the leaks to let some more of that old stuff out, so they make room for new learning."

The picture is now a mass of corrected dashes, but cat's point is made.

"Then they'd always have a bucket of fresh learning, instead of the remains of their old learning."

He lets out a deep and prolonged sigh as he adds.

'What did you ask at school today?' Richard Feynman

"People, they know lots, but then again they know little."

Turning towards donkey, cat points a claw at the scratched sketch to draw his attention to it and explains.

"It doesn't matter how much you've got in your bucket. How much you're pouring in, that's what matters, and I'd say donkey that you've just started to open up the tap."

Journeys

Beetle has been waiting to offer his words of support.

"Changing our lives is both fabulous and difficult, but that difficulty lives mostly in our heads. Once you accept that it's difficult, then it starts to begin. Remember difficult means possible, and possible means it will be done. When it is done, don't look for a big day, or a special event, or wait for special people. It happens on normal days, in the quiet moments, and the special people will be you and I."

'I am somehow less interested in the weight and convolutions of Einstein's brain, than in the near certainty that people of equal talent have lived and died in cotton fields and sweatshops.' Stephen Jay Gould

Donkey liked the idea of being special. It wasn't a feeling that he was used to. It wasn't a feeling he could ever remember having before.

He could see that change felt much like his journeys hauling supplies; scale a peak and the next minute you're down a ravine. He had seen highs and lows, felt lost and the next moment that being lost was being found. 'Maybe without the ravines, you just can't have peaks', he thought. This was a journey, but a new one, one the like of which he hadn't experienced before.

However, donkey could not suppress the feeling of inferiority in the face of beetle and cat's knowledge.

"Where did you learn so much? You couldn't have learned it from people."

"Oh we learned plenty from people," answered cat.

Donkey looked puzzled as cat's description had begun to undermine his previously high regard for the cleverness of people, reducing them to little more than leaky buckets.

"Remember, learning can be of 'how to' and of 'how not to'. Sometimes 'how not to' is the most powerful sort of learning," continued cat to help unravel yet another paradox in donkey's mind.

People

"And you can learn a lot of 'how not to' from people" added beetle with a grin.

"In fact if you want to learn how not to learn, then people's the best place to look." agreed cat with a vigorous nod of his head.

Then as if the nod had served to awaken a new idea he added,

"Did I tell you about the time I lived with people? No, well let me tell you. Oh they were nice, don't get me wrong. They provided me with everything they thought I needed. If I didn't fancy what they'd got me to eat, all I had to do was turn my head in a disdainful way."

'You are the person who has to decide. Whether you'll do it or toss it aside; you are the person who makes up your mind. Whether you'll lead or will linger behind. Whether you'll try for the goal that's afar. Or just be contented to stay where you are.' Edgar A. Guest

Cat demonstrated turning his head with a level of disdain that drew gasps from his audience.

"Yes I'd give them that look and straight away they'd make me something different, and again and again. Sometimes I'd let them make me five or six different meals and wouldn't touch any, especially if I'd already eaten out."

Cat winked mischievously before continuing.

"You see that was the point, they kept giving me meals that they thought I should want. If I brought home what I really wanted, you know something I'd caught fresh, they'd go crazy, chase me and throw it out and then give me their food. They always thought they knew the answer. They had their view, their plans and everything had to fit in."

'One must be a god to be able to tell successes from failures without making a mistake.' Anton Pavlovich Chekhov

Cat paused relishing the attention, and the lack of interruption served as his cue to continue with the story.

"One time they built a cat flap. They said they built it for me; didn't ask me if I wanted one of course! They thought I was going to go through this 'iddy-biddy' little door. It didn't even swing the right way like a door."

"No?" offered donkey.

"No. It was more like the lid on a waste bin, swinging at the top,"

A limp wave of a paw to mimic its movement and cat's expression underline his contempt for the very idea.

"And they expected me to go through that. Boy do they fail to understand cool! So I ignored this little flap and just kept scratching at the door to be let in. They thought I hadn't got it. Then they tried pushing me through the hole. Of course the more they pushed the more I resisted, scratching and snarling, I gave them the works."

'I prepared excitedly for my departure, as if this journey had a mysterious significance. I had decided to change my mode of life. "'til now," I told myself, "you have only seen the shadow and been well content with it; now, I am going to lead you into the substance.'
Nikos Kazantzakis

"Then what happened?" asked donkey intrigued at the thought of the contest between cat and people, and in no doubt that cat would be an impressive sight when giving them 'the works'.

"Well they put food the other side of the door, to tempt me to go through. If it was tuna or chicken I just reached through and scooped it out to eat. They really didn't get it. They thought they were teaching me! I learned how to get the food, how to stop them pushing me through the flap, how to get them to open the door by scratching and wailing till they could stand no more, and they thought they were teaching me!"

Donkey and beetle laughed as cat gave an impromptu rendition of his wailing.

"They learned nothing. In fact they learned less than nothing. They went away convinced that I couldn't use the cat flap and that I was stupid. Now that riled me a little. I know it shouldn't and it's not cool, but just a little it riled me in to one last attempt to teach them."

"What did you do?" chorused an intrigued beetle and donkey.

"Well one day, when they had all but given up on the cat flap and were planning to seal it up, I waited until they were all in the kitchen eating. I even rubbed up against their legs just to let them know I was there. Then I went out through the cat flap turned around and straight back in. They all saw it, started shouting and pointing and making a commotion. Just that once. I never did it again and they still couldn't learn that I knew all about cat flaps. They just all agreed that this confirmed that I was stupid."

Donkey laughed and nodded at this seemingly damning evidence of people's inability to learn.

Answers

"People, they've got their knowledge and their ideas, but they just don't seem able to learn somehow," continued cat. "Anyway then they decided not to seal the cat flap, just in case I used it again. So now I get to use it for emergencies when they aren't at home, and I make sure that I never let them see me." Cat shakes his head and adds, "Think they are teaching me, a cat, the grand master of change!"

Content that his point has been well made, cat has one last stretch before he lays himself down, ready to rest.

'I have learnt silence from the talkative, toleration from the intolerant, and kindness from the unkind; yet strangely, I am ungrateful to these teachers.'
Kahlil Gibran

"That's just it with people," beetle adds, "they're not ready to learn. For people change is a competition. It's them versus the change, a battle. If it's a change they want, they force it. If it's change they don't want, they see it as a threat, something to avoid, something to deny."

To emphasise his point beetle prods at the ground.

"Even on this little mountain change is inevitable, even the rocks beneath our feet are changing with the seasons, with each shower of rain, with every footstep on them. Change, learning and mistakes are part of what is all around us."

Donkey scans to the horizon, remembering his earlier thoughts of a brand new world every day, and again feels a tremor as the earth moves beneath his hooves.

'Traditional scientific method has always been at the very best, 20 - 20 hindsight. It's good for seeing where you've been. It's good for testing the truth of what you think you know, but it can't tell you where you ought to go.'
Robert M. Pirsig

"People see everything as win or lose and they think they control everything, including the future. They build their plans and when they work they call it success and think they were so clever."

"And when they don't they call it failure and look for something to blame." interrupts cat, postponing his sleep for a moment.

"That's right. They don't realise that they don't, you can't, control the future. What they call 'success' when it happens, just means they guessed what would happen reasonably well, and 'failure' they guessed it wrong, both are the result of the same process of guessing."

"They guess?" asks donkey almost incredulously as the previously incontestable powers of people continue to be peeled from them like the layers from an onion.

"Oh they make educated guesses, expensive guesses where they agonise and compute. They look to history and experience. They mimic what may have worked in other situations from the past. But what they can't see is that the past is no more. They are busy changing it with their right hand whilst relying on it being the same, for their calculations and predictions, with their left.

It's crazy and can only make sense to folk who have forgotten all about real learning."

"And learning is change," donkey adds from his own new learning.

Dreaming

An image comes to cat's mind and he quickly butts in to share it.

"They are like a man I once saw on the farm I stayed on. He was sawing through a branch on a tree, the very same branch he was standing on to saw! Even when it creaked and started to bend, he didn't realise. Not until he was dumped on the ground did he understand that he'd removed a piece of the past he was relying on."

Cat executes an elegant and prolonged fall to underline the story. From his prone position he concludes much to the laughter of the others, "If you are creating change, the future can't possibly be like the past. And even if you aren't creating change, somebody near you certainly is."

"It's like we saw with the sheepdog," adds beetle. "If you are barking at the sheep, pretty soon they aren't going to be where they were! So knowing where they were is no good to you, but nor is knowing where you planned them to be. Knowing how to learn where they've gone, that's what you need. What holds people back is not knowing how to really learn"

"You are right. They just don't seem to know the value of learning" adds cat. "Why, if we tried to tell people what we've told you donkey, what would they say? I'll tell you. They'd say ok cat, if you're so clever at understanding change, why do you spend so much time asleep, dreaming? Why don't you use that time usefully instead of wasting it?"

'There is more to life than increasing its speed.'
Mahatma Gandhi

Wide eyed in exaggerated astonishment, cat adds, "Can you see how they just don't understand?"

Donkey wasn't yet ready to confess that he hadn't really understood where sleep and dreaming fitted into cat's capabilities, and was relieved that a nod was enough to set cat off again.

"You see they don't understand learning. People think that learning is finding something that worked, and doing it again and again, only this time bigger and faster, then bigger and faster still, and on and on. Can you imagine what would happen if the sheepdog misunderstood like that?"

Cat enjoyed acting out the actions of the sheepdog as he continued his description.

"Imagine the first time he walks into the field of sheep and does something that gets the sheep moving, say a little yap. He sees the sheep move, so yap, yap, now bigger and faster YAP, YAP, YAP, YAP, in just a few minutes he's bellowing at the top of his bark and it's pandemonium."

Beetle and donkey, clearly impressed with cat's mimicry, egg him on to continue.

'Imagination is more important than knowledge, for while knowledge points to all there is, imagination points to all there will be.' Albert Einstein.

"Even the sheepdog, a dog for heavens sake, even the sheepdog knows that isn't learning. People are so obsessed with doing, with answers, with solutions that work, that they completely miss the point." Cat's raised eyebrows emphasise his exasperation.

He takes a deep breath and a stretch to regain his composure. "Even the dog takes a little time to reflect on his yap, only a little time, but we're talking about dogs remember. When he reflects he thinks and he imagines, not what could I do the same, but what could I do *differently*. He imagines questions, not answers! People can't see this."

Looking to the heavens and in a disbelieving tone cat adds, "And they ask why we waste our time dreaming."

Like an episode of a mystery serial, donkey hangs on cat's words, again waiting for the importance of dreaming to be fully revealed.

"Dreaming…?" he asks.

Fortunately again cat needs little prompting,

"Dreaming. Dreaming is the realm of the imagination. The opportunity to dream is the reward for learning, and the place that creates the next learning. Whilst people seek to mass produce the past with what they mistakenly call learning, if they only allowed themselves the time to think and to dream, they could be creating the future."

'No amount of sophistication is going to allay the fact, that all your knowledge is about the past, and all your decisions are about the future.' Ian E. Wilson

Donkey was struck by the phrase 'creating the future'. 'Each day is a brand new day', he thought to himself, 'a brand new day and a place to create brand new days, a place to create the future.'

From somewhere he recalled half heard words that beetle had said earlier, 'no reason why tomorrow need be like today'.

Eyes

"Cat's right, people value doing, not dreaming." beetle adds in support. "You see people are so afraid of not doing. They prefer the sound of doing, doing anything at all, to the silence of thinking. They don't understand dreaming as part of change and part of being. For them the future is described in plans – the fixed plan of the ineffective sheepdog setting out to bark out his commands. They've turned the wonderful expansive magic of dreaming into the mechanical closed plodding of doing plans, plans based on what they already know; the past!. The soaring eagle confined to a cage."

'Great things are not accomplished by those who yield to trends and fads and popular opinion.'
Charles Kuralt

Donkey nods vigorously to confirm that he now perfectly understands where dreaming fits in cat's capabilities. Again he'd been looking but not seeing.

Meanwhile beetle continues to share his understanding, and in doing so, his dismantling of people's ability to really learn.

"People just can't see. They don't know the difference between folk who've become change, and those who don't even appreciate the need. They both look the same to people – asleep. So people can only recognise this in-between state, of being busy doing. They tell the difference by what folk do, because they can't see what folk are."

Like a passed relay baton, cat takes over the assault.

"They look at the hands when they should be looking into the eyes. That's where you need to look to see what someone is and to learn about change. That's why we cat's sleep, why we've developed senses that give us the space to dream and imagine."

As if prompted by the thought, cat revels in a luxurious yawn before continuing.

"When you do change right, you earn time to dream, and dreaming is the way to do change right. People are too obsessed with doing things directly; they don't have the subtlety to understand the power of the indirect."

'If a little dreaming is dangerous, the cure for it is not to dream less but to dream more, to dream all the time.' Marcel Proust

Cat pauses for a moment to let a new series of images form in his mind's eye.

"If people ever understood this stuff they could achieve some great things, but it will never happen, and do you know why I'm so sure?"

Once again in his excitement to convey the message, cat is in no mood to wait for a response.

"As soon as they start to change they're looking to call it success or failure. If it's failure they throw it away and start again, but success is even worse. If they call it success then they waste their dreaming time on doing more of what they have; more of the same, faster, bigger but the same. As soon as they move, they stop looking for something that will move them, and hang on to what *did* move them. They just can't help themselves holding onto the past. They don't even realise they are doing it.

'Dreaming is an act of pure imagination, attesting in all men a creative power, which if it were available in waking, would make every man a Dante or Shakespeare.'
H.F. Hedge

Cat pauses and reflects for a moment.

"That's why we never have to worry that people will get this stuff. They have no real understanding of how important it is to create space, to allow time, to think and then to dream and imagine."

Donkey's expression reveals that he can hardly believe this picture of people, as he clings to the vestiges of what he's seen of people's achievements.

Beetle sensing this adds.

"Oh its true people have achieved some impressive things, but who knows what they might have achieved. As cat says, they get so excited at the first successful bark, content that something happened, they just bark again louder and louder thinking that's improvement."

'To achieve something beyond your wildest dreams, you'd better have some wild dreams.'
Anon

"But what about the machines and buildings they've made?" Donkey asks, aware of the things that people have achieved. He's seen some of them, the ferocious noise of the machines that help them burrow into the mountain, the buildings the miners live in, and he's heard them talk of many more.

"Oh they look impressive, but they don't realise what they could have achieved, and seldom leave space to ask the question," replies beetle. "They spend most of their time in a stupor, a kind of suspended animation. It's as if they have the opposite to cat's ability. For people, they can't see change, they only see the static. They miss what's happening and only see what they planned to happen."

Bicycle

Beetle's antennae explore a water swollen seed pod washed from a tree as he continues,

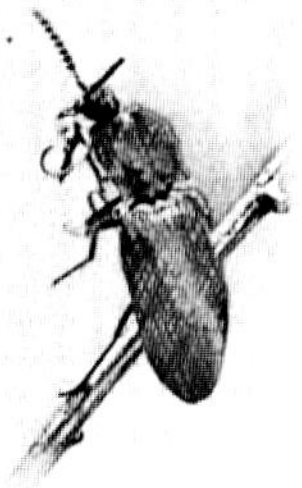

"Change isn't about doing things, mechanical things, unthinking things, not even the things people call progress. These might help people convince themselves that they are committed to change, even that they are changing, by giving them something to do. But they just create a comforting noise that people choose to call progress."

Beetle's face breaks into a big smile as an example comes to mind.

"Take your handler for instance donkey. He's a little overweight."

Donkey pulls a face in response.

"Ok, so he's a lot overweight, so what does he do?"

"Joins the gym?" replied donkey after a moment's thought.

"That's right he joins the gym. Then he decides he hasn't the time to go. So he buys an exercise bicycle and then within a week he decides he hasn't the space to ride it. He wants to take exercise and lose weight, and these things look so much like the right thing to do, but often are so much the wrong thing to do."

"Well they should help," offers donkey.

"Yes, they could help, but if he wants to get fit, first he has to change his thinking. Only then does the gym or the exercise bicycle make any sense. If his thinking isn't right, there'll be a thousand things that will stop him from using them."

'Don't measure yourself by what you have accomplished, but by what you should have accomplished with your ability.' John Wooden

Cat adds, "And once his thinking is right he might find he doesn't need the bicycle, because he starts to walk more and eat the right foods, and do lots of other things automatically that make him fitter, and help his weight go down. His focus is on being fit, not on doing exercise."

"Like the sheepdog." offers donkey. "He no longer sees the gym or the exercise bicycle. Now he sees the change in his body, just like the sheepdog saw the change in the flock."

"Exactly" agrees beetle, "All change has to start with this thinking. The actions then take care of themselves."

Contentment

Donkey feels a sense of contentment, a sense of achievement. If change starts with thinking, then his change has indeed begun. His ship has begun to break free of the ice.

He looks across to see cat as he begins his own exercise programme, engaging in yet another luxurious stretch as a prelude to finding the perfect spot for a nap.

Beetle kicks a small ball of dirt as he continues to kick over thoughts in his head, before sharing them.

"The problem with most people is they dread having to think. They have the biggest, most powerful brain you could imagine, but they act as if they are always saving it for tomorrow."

Donkey laughs at the idea of saving your brain, as beetle continues.

"They'll avoid using their brain and instead look for something to do. They'll adopt any manner of quack remedy, just so long as they can start to 'do' without having to think. It's the strangest thing. If they took the trouble to find out how much we achieve with our little brains, they'd surely expect to achieve more with theirs."

Donkey can't help feeling a little guilty when he thinks of his brain compared to beetle's, or even cat's.

"I think maybe people have too much brain." offers cat, postponing his nap once more.

"How can that be, too much brain?" As he asks, donkey quietly thinks to himself 'maybe that's my problem too.'

"Well they have so much that they think they can understand everything, know everything, but even with their big brains it's not possible to know everything about everything."

"Or everything about anything" adds beetle.

Break-up

"Exactly. So they break things up into smaller pieces. They make things small enough that they can think they know everything, but by breaking it up they make sure that they know nothing. It's like they try to round up the sheep one at a time, because one feels manageable. They deal with a single sheep but then can't even see or recognise the flock. They deal in sheep, but no matter how much you know about the portion, you know nothing about the whole, and the whole is the reality."

'If you see a whole thing - it seems that it's always beautiful. Planets, lives.... But close up a world's all dirt and rocks. And day to day, life's a hard job, you get tired, you lose the pattern.' Ursula K. Leguin

Cat's input again leaves donkey a little unsure, and his puzzled look prompts cat to continue his explanation.

"Well, the more you look into the sheep, the less you see it as part of the flock. And just like the flock, the real world is a wildly connected place that is constantly changing, with each change creating cascades of further change. The world's not a collection of pieces that will each stand still whilst you deal with just one of them."

"You're right cat," says beetle "It's not only things, but the connections between them that make up the world. Instead of cutting things up to learn all about the piece, people need to stand back and see what's really there and what's really happening."

Beetle's antennae continue to flick around as he adds, "Standing back is something you learn to do if you only have a small brain."

He taps his head as if the small size of his brain needs to be pointed out to the other two. "There's no point me trying to understand the detail of a rock, if I'm not also checking for holes, looking for food, watching for birds. I'd know all about the rock and the inside of a bird's stomach before too long if I did that."

The expression of donkey's face reveals that he sees this as a disturbing prospect, but beetle just laughs as he continues, "I stand back far enough to know what I need about the real total picture, not as much as I possibly can about a small part of it. If you stand back and see the whole flock, it becomes much easier to understand than it is to know everything about a single strand of wool on a sheep's back."

Donkey thinks about not knowing and begins to create a list of all the things he doesn't know about a strand of wool. He imagines for a moment the immensity of his not knowing, and the power of standing back. As he lets his mind wander he enjoys a mouthful of grass and muses. "My uncle used to work on the beach."

"The beach?" asks beetle, unsure as to where this might lead.

"Yes. Carrying children, you know back and forth along the beach." He beams a wry smile towards beetle as he adds, "Or round and round. Anyway, he always said the beach was a great place to stand back. He said the sea makes you have to stand back and recognise how small you are."

"I guess so." beetle nods.

"Funny thing though. He always said, being small doesn't mean you can't achieve big things."

He pauses to think for a moment before adding,

"I never really understood before, but he used to say being small was the way to achieve big things. I think I now know what he meant."

'Only as high as I reach can I grow,
Only as far as I seek can I go,
Only as deep as I look can I see,
Only as much as I dream can I be.'
Karen Ravn

Donkey pieces together the different pictures of people painted by cat and beetle. He recognises that much of his own thinking was described in these pictures. Though he hoped to leave this thinking behind, he feels bruised from the effort of separating the old from new in his mind. He takes the chance to seek out a fresh clump of grass to munch on as he lets his thoughts collect once more. As he savours the smell and the taste of the fresh grass, the challenge he faces crystallises in his mind.

"Taking control by letting go, that feels nearly impossible."

Being

Cat had taken the opportunity to do a little more pre nap personal cleaning, and was in the middle of a particularly satisfying stretch. His claws dug deep into the bark of a tree from which he carefully extracts himself before answering,

"You're right, but that's only how it feels when you are holding on tightly. It's at the very heart of change."

Donkey thought for a moment, before asking, "Holding on to what?"

"The past" cat says emphatically. "People think change is something you can pull on a rope. They like to pull things on ropes. I blame dogs a lot for that. But the future is out in front of us. The rope doesn't work when you push it out in front. So most people keep on pulling on the past and calling it the future. They avoid change, real change, by taking a bit of the past and tugging it into the future. Oh they dress it up in all kinds of fancy ways, but it's still just a bit of the past they've dragged along. If they'd only open their minds so they can see what could be, rather than just what has been, they'd see the future is a place of real magic."

'You can become blind by seeing each day as a similar one. Each day is a different one, each day brings a miracle of its own. It's just a matter of paying attention to this miracle.'
Paulo Coelho,

That word again. Donkey liked the word 'magic'. He'd heard it a lot in their discussions. It was a word he'd never before used to describe his life. It had never felt appropriate. Indeed it had felt so inappropriate that the thought would have been absurd. But now he could conceive of using the word. It had an exciting feel to it, and he felt intoxicated by the thought of the future, his future being exciting, even magical.

" It's a place not created by control, but by being brave enough to enable things to happen, and leaving the space to let it take place." Cat said finishing his description.

There were longer pauses now between the inputs from each of them. More reflection, more thinking and imagining. Within a few minutes cat is sprawled in the warmth of the sun, asleep but of course paying close attention. Beetle, antennae twitching checks and rechecks the earth around him, choosing to move position to a new driest spot, whilst donkey chews on grass as he looks into the distance down the valley towards the sheep farm.

"It's what we do with our children" says donkey reflecting on a memory that comes to mind.

Cat's ears swivel, but it's beetle who asks, "What's that?"

'Life is not lost by dying; life is lost minute by minute, day by dragging day, in all the thousand small uncaring ways.' Stephen Vincent Benét

"Our children. If we've done a good job of enabling them, when we've set them free they go on to achieve..., well who knows what they might achieve."

Donkey is still reliving these memories as cat and beetle nod in agreement.

For the next few minutes no one speaks. They seem to have shared so much that it takes some time for each of them to order their thoughts. Donkey is the first to break the silence.

"Now I understand how you learned so much."

Beetle breaks off from the examination of a small mound of drying leaf litter and adds, "Well there is one way that's even more important."

"There is?"

Donkey isn't sure he has space for more learning, but beetle presses on anyway.

"Yes, just by being."

Cat sits up, hesitating as if to savour the comment, then says. "I like that beetle. Yes, I guess that's right, 'just by being says it all."

He pauses for a moment creating a picture in his mind conjured up by those three words, and then continues as if inspired by this picture.

"If you are open to it, there is learning all around you in every moment of every day. It's just there waving its hands, screaming for you to take notice. If you can see it, then it's not just a tap there available to fill your bucket, it's a flood. There's just a torrent of learning everywhere you tread."

He lowers his head as he continues, "But if you don't see it, then there's nothing, and no one can point it out to you. You are just plain blind. There's no use pointing to more of it, or pouring it in a dish in front of you, or even hosing you down with it. If you can't see it then there's no point doing anything at all, but working on your seeing."

Cat stretches again and looks up to the sky as he continues.

"It's just like this sunny day. You feel the heat and hear the crickets, you smell the flowers and see colour, bright colour in every direction. For some folk it's like your senses have just been switched on. But the sounds, smells, sights are all here in the dead of winter. Different sights, different sounds, but here. The sound of crumpling snow or dripping rain. The smell of frost or damp leaves. The sight of frozen droplets on a leaf with their tiny rainbows of colour. They're all here to be sensed, and if you don't, it's not your senses that have been switched off, it's your thinking, your learning."

'The air is full of ideas. They are knocking you in the head all the time. You only have to know what you want, then forget it, and go about your business. Suddenly, the idea will come through. It was there all the time.' Henry Ford

Cat extends his body, and his stretch seems itself to be an act of gathering up armfuls of learning, "Yes learning is all around if you are here to see it, and with the learning there's opportunity."

They pause almost as if all three of them have become aware of how much learning surrounds them.

Stretch

"And don't go thinking that beetle and I have learned so much. We might know a little more than you, but just like you we're on a journey. Some of that journey we'll make, and some we'll pass on. It's like a chain that reaches right into the future and back into the past, and we're just a link.

People have a special word for it... in... in?" Cat struggles to recall the word. Beetle obliges.

"Infinity!"

"Infinity, that's it. Fancy that, a special word and they still forget what it means. They let themselves think that they're the last or only link. They think that they've got it right, their understanding, or have got to get it right, or can ever get it right. They fail to realise that there's no such thing as right. Instead they should make things better, that's their link in the chain, making things a little better. Infinite learning behind us and infinite learning ahead," cat mused.

"Infinity and the future... what you said the other day beetle." Donkey strains to recall the precise words. "You said a world that doesn't

'We are at the very beginning of time for the human race. It is not unreasonable that we grapple with problems. But there are tens of thousands of years in the future. Our responsibility is to do what we can, learn what we can, improve the solutions, and pass them on.
Richard P. Feynman.

exist. Taking things that worked in a world that no longer exists"

"Yes"

"Well asking questions, that's the key. If you ask questions, then there's the space to create a brand new world, whatever you want."

"Whatever you can imagine" adds cat.

Donkey had never felt this way before. It was like he'd been stretched in every sense. His mind had been extended like a canvas across a frame, pulled taut in every direction. His confidence had been pulled in one direction to new heights and in another to new depths. He felt he knew so much, but what he knew was how little he knew. He had learned, but what he had learned was only the beginning of learning to learn. When things feel good, they are probably bad, and when things feel bad, it's the start of them getting good. When cat's asleep he's really awake, but people awake are often asleep.

'If we could see the miracle of a single flower clearly, our whole life would change.'
Buddha

He'd been contented, or thought he was contented before, but now he couldn't conceivably understand how. It's as if the canvas had previously been crumpled into a small ball, so tightly that he had barely known it was there. He knew now that it could only grow by being stretched ever further, and was the canvas on which he could paint his future. There was no going back.

'In the end, it is the person you become, not the things you have achieved, that is the most important.' Les Brown

Donkey could see his handler approaching to lead him down to the stables.

"You're looking a bit better old lad. Perhaps we won't be needing the vet after all. What was it? Did you just need some time to rest?"

The handler patted him fondly on his neck.

'Yes, just a little time to think and dream, that's all', thought donkey.

'Man's mind, once stretched by a new idea, never regains its original dimensions.' Oliver Wendell Holmes

Whilst the handler was untangling the rope with which he'd lead him down the mountain, donkey thanked beetle and cat.

"Let's hope the sun shines tomorrow and we can talk some more"

"Sure, but don't forget the learning there is even if it rains," answered cat.

"Even if it rains." Donkey smiled.

He had learned lots and knew he had much more to learn on other days. However there was one last question that didn't feel as if it would wait.

"This thing that's all together – what you've called change and learning, questions, not knowing and making mistakes, all joined

'You can't get there by bus, only by hard work and risk and by not quite knowing what you're doing. What you'll discover will be wonderful. What you'll discover will be yourself.'
Alan Alda

together so one thing becomes the next. What's the whole thing called?"

"Well that's a very fine question, perhaps the finest question of all, and the answer is the real secret," said cat.

He took one luxuriant lick of his paw before adding, "I call it life."

'Have the courage to live. Anyone can die.'
Robert Cody

The Journey

If you measure how long it's taken,
you missed the point.
If you're waiting for magic,
you've missed the spell.
If you're expecting to be told,
you must have misheard.
But if you are ready to go,
you're already half way there.

Steve Unwin

Fellow Travellers

The quotations have been chosen for what was said, not who said it.

Over the past few years I've collected many hundreds, perhaps thousands of quotations, each chosen because I felt a resonance in the words.

Pursuing your own thoughts can sometimes be a lonely journey. To think differently you face the challenge perfectly described by Albert Einstein.

"A question that sometimes drives me hazy: am I or are the others crazy?"

The collected quotations often seemed to offer the outstretched hand of a fellow traveller, lessening the loneliness of the journey.

Strangely I began to notice that often the quotations would come to my attention just as they were needed. Stranger still, though each had been carefully collected, when the moment came it felt as if the quotation were being seen for the first time.

It was as if my right brain had been colleting them knowing that they would be of value on future steps of the journey. It was some time later before they made sense and were able to be seen by my logical left brain.

One can't help but feel that our intuition knows the nature of the journey ahead. We have to wait for life to play out before it is revealed to our logic.

I hope that the quotations offer you the same guiding hands of the fellow traveller.

Quotations

Page	Traveller	
vii	Chief Seattle	Leader of the Suquamish and Duwamish Native American Indian tribes. 1786 - 1866
x	Helen Keller	Deaf blind author, activist and lecturer 1880-1968
9	Pablo Picasso	Spanish painter and sculptor, 1881-1973
9	Andrew Jackson	Seventh President of the United States 1829-1837
10	Carl Sagan	Astronomer, astrobiologist, science popularizer 1934 – 1996
11	Albert Szent-Györgyi	Nobel prize winning physiologist 1893 - 1986
12	Christina Baldwin	Spiritual speaker and educator
14	Joan Didion	Writer, journalist, essayist and novelist, born 1934
15	Virginia Woolf	Feminist modernist author, 1882 – 1941
17	John Fowles	Author of The French Lieutenant's Woman 1926 – 2005
19	Jim Rohn	Author, Business Coach & Motivational Speaker
22	Bette Howland	Jewish American writer.
23	Trinidad Hunt	Author and writer
23	Anais Nin	Modernist writer, 1903 – 1977
30	Madeleine L'Engle	Adult and children's book author, born 1918

32	John Seely Brown	Chief Scientist of Xerox Corporation
35	Alan Alda	Oscar nominated actor, born 1936
37	William James	Psychologist and philosopher, 1842 – 1910
40	Alan Cohen	Writer and poet, 1940 - 2004
49	Pythagoras	Greek mathematician, 569-475 B.C.
52	Martin Luther King	Civil rights leader, 1929 – 1968
53	Bruce Barton	Advertising executive, writer, congressman 1886 – 1967
54	G.K. Chesterton	Influential writer known as Prince of Paradox 1874 – 1936
58	Niels Bohr	Nobel prize winning quantum physicist 1885 – 1962
61	Wu-Men (Hui-K'ai)	Head monk of the Lung-hsiang monastery in China. 1183 – 1260
62	Denis Waitley	Personal development speaker
64	Leonardo Da Vinci	Artist, sculptor, engineer, scientist, architect 1452 – 1519
66	Paul Hawken	Environmentalist, entrepreneur, journalist, author.
69	William James	Psychologist and philosopher, 1842 – 1910
70	Frank Dick	Sports Coach

71	Ovid	Roman poet, BC 43-18 AD
73	Peter Vaill	Writer on the subject of learning
77	Lau Tzu	Founder of Taoism, c. 600 BC
78	Doug King	
80	Frederick August Hayek	Austrian economist, 1899 – 1992
82	Euripides	Greek playwright and revolutionary tragedian 480 - 406 BC
85	Lewis Caroll	Author, mathematician, clergyman, photographer 1832 – 1898
86	Henry B. Adams	Historian, political biographer, philosopher 1838 – 1918
88	John Anthony Ciardi	Poet, translator, etymologist, 1916 – 1986
89	Paulo Coelho	Brazilian lyricist and novelist, born 1947.
94	Peter Senge	Writer on organisational learning, MIT lecturer.
97	Kahlil Gibran	Lebanese born artist, poet, writer, 1883 – 1931
105	Kathleen Norris	American novelist
108	Rachael Snyder	Author
109	Lau Tzu	Founder of Taoism, c 600 BC
110	Richard Feynman	Nobel prize winning physicist, 1918 - 1988
111	Earl Gray Stevens	

113	Ralph Waldo Emerson	Poet and philosopher 1803 – 1882
119	Mary Richards	
121	C.S. Lewis	Writer and critic 1898 – 1963
124	Alan Alda	Oscar nominated actor, born 1936
126	André Gide	French Nobel prize winning writer, 1869 – 1951
130	Mary Anne Radmacher	Author
132	Richard Feynman	Nobel Prize Winning Physicist 1918 – 1988
133	Stephen J Gould	
135	Edgar A Guest	Poet 1881 – 1959
135	Anton Chekhov	Physician, writer, playwright, 1860 – 1904
136	Nikos Kazantzakis	Greek writer and philosopher, 1883 – 1957
138	Kahlil Gibran	Lebanese born artist, poet, writer, 1883 – 1931
139	Robert M Pirsig	Philosopher, writer, Author Zen and the Art of Motorcycle Maintenance, born 1928
141	Mahatma Gandhi	Indian political and spiritual leader 1869 – 1948
142	Albert Einstein	Physicist, mathematician, 1879 – 1955
143	Ian E Wilson	Librarian and archivist
144	Charles Kuralt	American TV commentator

145	Marcel Proust	French intellectual, novelist, essayist and critic, 1871 – 1922
146	H F Hedge	
148	John Robert Wooden	Basketball Coach, born 1910
151	Ursula K Leguin	Writer of science fiction and fantasy, born 1929
153	Karen Ravn	Children's writer
154	Paulo Coelho	Brazilian lyricist and novelist, born 1947.
155	Stephen Vincent Benét	Author, novelist, poet, 1898 – 1943
157	Henry Ford	Founder of the Ford motor company, 1863 – 1947
159	Richard Feynman	Nobel Prize Winning Physicist 1918 – 1988
159	Buddha	Founder of Buddhism, 560 – 480 BC
160	Les Brown	Motivational speaker and author, born 1945
160	Oliver Wendell Holmes	Member US Supreme Court, 1841 - 1935
161	Alan Alda	Oscar nominated actor, born 1936
162	Robert Cody	
165	Albert Einstein	Physicist, mathematician, 1879 - 1955

Steve Unwin

About the Author

Steve has a background as a chartered engineer. After 10 years spent developing software systems for the aerospace industry he turned his systems thinking towards organisational improvement, working with the European Foundation for Quality Management on the development of improvement tools.

He played a key role in the transformation of the UK based aerospace business and in 1999 he jointly received the prestigious UK Excellence Award from HRH The Princess Royal in recognition of this work.

Since 2001 he has focused on personal and human aspects of change. He is recognised as an insightful and inspiring speaker at conferences worldwide and delivers individual and corporate change consultancy.

The following pages outline some of Steve's other titles available from photonbooks.com

Steve lives in the city of Preston in the UK with his family of three children.

To find out more please visit
www.steveunwin.com
www.photonbooks.com

Other titles from photonbooks.com

Travellers.

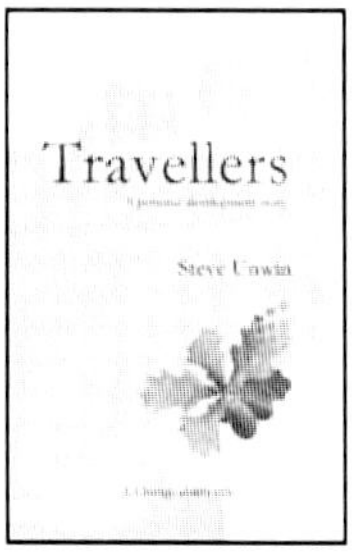

ISBN 978-1-906420-01-7

'Travellers' explores the contrast between a world seen through questions and one seen through answers. It reveals the impact of the different paradigms we may inhabit and through which we see and understand our world.

Complete with over 80 carefully selected quotations to stimulate new trains of thought, this is a catalyst for change.

Essence of Da Vinci

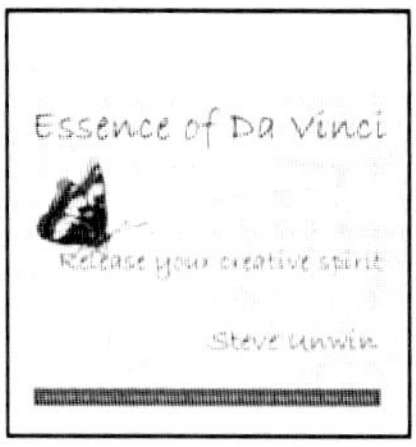

ISBN 978-1-906420-02-4

Inspired by Leonardo Da Vinci's thinking style, this insightful and wide ranging collection of quotations, taken from more modern times, illustrates the impact of creative genius in all walks of life. Supported by specially created drawings, the quotations serve to inspire the creative soul that lurks within all of us.

Featuring over 100 drawings and 250 quotations this is a treasury of insightful prompts to a more creative life.

Himalayan Odyssey

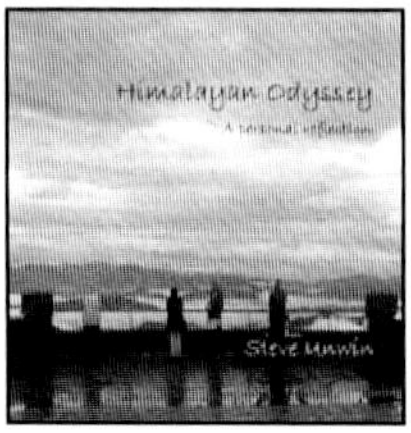

ISBN 978-1-906420-03-1

A collection of thought provoking quotations and sketches inspired by a gathering of special people in the Himalayan mountains of Nepal.

With delegates from 15 countries, 'Asian Camp' shared and explored the latest ideas on creating successful change. Himalayan Odyssey enchantingly captures the spirit of the gathering. With nearly 100 quotations and over 100 specially created drawings, it shares and inspires new thinking and change.

Essence of Excellence

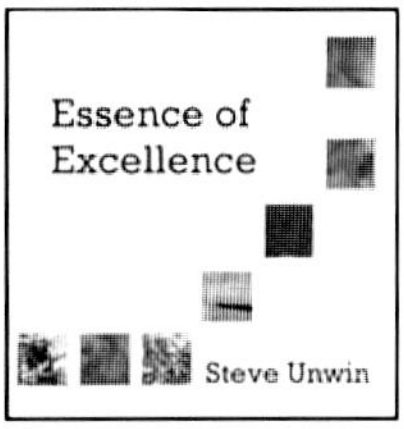

ISBN 978-1-906420-05-5

This book is an antidote to those that claim to provide instructions for excellence.

Rather than list best practice from the past, this collection of quotations is designed to inspire the creation of the best practices of the future.

With over 180 carefully selected quotations and 130 drawings this is a book to inspire excellence in individuals and organisations.

Iran Inspired

ISBN 978-1-906420-07-9

A special collection of quotations and drawings that capture some of the essence of Iran, it's people and history.

Over 120 carefully selected quotations and more than 100 drawings, create a powerful prompt for new ideas.

Beyond Best Practice - Available Soon

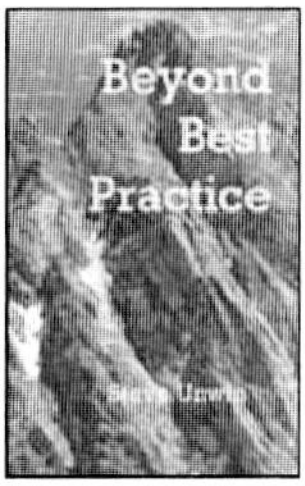

'.... all your knowledge is about the past and all of your questions are about the future.'

In 'Beyond Best Practice' we explore what it takes to survive and succeed in a world where the ground continuously moves from beneath your feet.

For news and special offers please visit photonbooks.com.

Corporate editions also available. A great way to energise your change program. See web site for details.